The Bible Uncomplicated

A Christian Business Case for Why We Believe

James Finke

MORE BOOKS BY JAMES FINKE

H AVE YOU READ THE ENTIRE *CHRISTIANITY UNCOMPLI-CATED* SERIES?

This book distills and deciphers the evidence that the God of the Bible exists. Are you ready? Let's talk God.

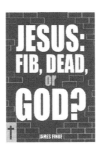

This book answers the most important question in history, asked by the most important person in history. Are you ready? Let's talk Jesus.

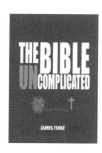

This book gives the business case for why we believe the Bible is the Word of God. Are you ready? Let's talk Bible.

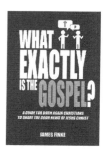

This book shares the most powerful message ever delivered on planet Earth. Let's talk Gospel.

JAMES FINKE READERS' CLUB

My free monthly email newsletter is packed with useful info to help you share the Good News of Jesus Christ with others. It contains deals and giveaways that aren't offered anywhere else, and you'll be the first to hear when new books in the series are released! Subscribers receive a welcome package that includes:

1. A free book of mine that is ONLY available to my readers' club.

2. A free audio download of the "You Don't Need a Ph.D. to Find G-O-D" message I delivered at my home church.

SUBSCRIBE

Contents

INTRODUCTION

I'm in the business of taking risks. Calculated risks. No, I'm not a poker player, a tightrope walker, or some sort of breathtaking acrobat at the circus. For fifteen years, I've worked as a Professional Liability Insurance Underwriter. We cover professionals against lawsuits that claim they made a mistake while performing their services. This is known as "errors and omissions" insurance, or E&O.

If that seems anticlimactic to you, you're in good company. It's the type of profession that almost invariably triggers a blank stare when brought up in conversation. But underwriters like me spend our days assessing risks and making multi-million dollar bets based on that research.

The term "underwriter" is said to have been coined in the 17th century at the world-famous Lloyds Coffee Shop in London. This coffee shop was frequented by many in the shipping industry and became the go-to location to obtain marine insurance. Risk-takers would write their name under the total amount of risk they were willing to accept for a specified fee. Hence the term, *underwriter*.

Then and now, the stakes can be very high. I specialize in underwriting companies that have, in their past, been sued for hundreds of thousands or millions of dollars.

What's more, a company doesn't necessarily need to have made a mistake to be sued. An old adage in our business goes, "All it takes is an unhappy client for a claim." For example, divorce attorneys get sued for negligence constantly – much more so than attorneys practicing other types of law. Are divorce attorneys a particularly negligent bunch? Do they make up the "C's get degrees" crowd at law schools? Of course not. The issue is that, almost by definition, the people hiring divorce attorneys are unhappy; and unhappy clients often sue their practitioners, especially professionals involved in nasty family disputes.

It's not glamorous, but business insurance like E&O is essential for a healthy economy. This is because we agree to take on a company's financial risk in exchange for a fee. Absent this risk transfer, companies would constantly be a lawsuit away from disaster. Indeed, even if a suit is dismissed in your favor, it could easily cost 5, 6, or 7 figures to defend.

I've wagered hundreds of millions of dollars on behalf of my employers throughout my career. These are calculated bets based on the meticulous evaluation of risk factors, and we've consistently produced a profit. But, perhaps even more important than the companies we've chosen to cover are the companies we've decided not to cover. If we lack confidence in a company, we may not participate or may only be willing to make a small wager until the company has proven itself.

In addition to the individual company assessments, we work diligently to maintain a broad and balanced portfolio. We're constantly monitoring our downside and ensuring we're not too heavily concentrated in any area. The whole idea is that we don't want any single deal to sink us, should it go wrong.

With all of this in mind, it may surprise you to know that I've gone all-in and wagered everything on the Bible.

Everything. My life is organized around it, and I've staked my eternity on the fact that it's true. In fact, billions of Christians have done so and will continue to do so every day. This is because we believe that the Bible truly, is the authoritative word of God.

So how does an analytical, risk-assessing, spreadsheet-loving insurance underwriter come to this conclusion? It's a reasonable question to ask, and we will walk through it together. The beautiful thing is, when something is correct, you can assess a wide range of factors, and they will all point to the truth. We'll look at how important the Bible is to the Christian faith and why we believe it's true. I'll provide you with some easy-to-remember information to help bolster your faith in a skeptical world. And we'll even dispose of some pesky, weak excuses that unbelievers lean on like, "I can't believe the Bible because it's been translated so many times."

Are you ready? Let's talk about why we believe the Bible.

Chapter One

TRIAGE

I work with a wonderful group of people – colleagues who are also friends. We understand that the well-being of our team essentially rests on who we choose to trust. Our livelihoods depend on it. We offer a promise to defend our clients if they get sued for negligence, and our company gets paid in exchange for that promise. We're tasked with choosing clients who in our careful evaluation, are the worthiest of our pledge to defend. If we pick the right clients, they don't get sued, and everybody's happy. If we choose wrong, the results can be ugly.

It sounds simple enough: find the best companies and only cover them. But when you realize just how large the pool of potential applicants is, the task of handpicking winners starts to feel like a "needle in a haystack" situation. Our team is "lean and mean," comprising of just 15 underwriters. Meanwhile, there are approximately 478,000 consulting firms, 48,000 law firms, 42,000 accounting firms, 36,000 insurance agencies, and 25,000 engineering firms in the US alone. In total, there are over 900,000 professional services firms in the US. So how does a team of 15 underwriters perform a careful evaluation of over 900,000 companies?

We can't.

And that's the point. Trying to learn everything there is to know about every potential client out there would be a huge strategic mistake. We have a finite amount of time and resources to work with. Every second we spend gathering superficial information on the wrong companies, we lose a second which we could've used to do a more thorough evaluation of the right company. So how do we address this?

We triage. Triage is defined as *assigning priority order to projects based on where funds and other resources can be best used, are most needed, or are most likely to achieve success*. People often hear this term being used in a medical setting. For instance, the patients in an emergency room are "triaged" based on the urgency of the care they need. The patient suffering a heart attack is going to be bumped up to the top of the priority list, even if the patient with a sprained ankle arrived earlier.

Triage is absolutely critical in my business too. We triage to quickly identify and eliminate the thousands of applicants that clearly aren't what we're looking for. Doing this efficiently frees us up to carefully evaluate the remaining firms that warrant a closer look.

Here's an example: most law firms in the country have only one or two attorneys on staff. However, our data (and experience) tell us that these firms have historically performed poorly for insurance companies. Without a triage process, a team like ours could waste all day evaluating these small firms that are unlikely to bring us success. It's a mismanagement of resources. To avoid this, we triage according to various eligibility requirements. In this case, firms with only 1 or 2 attorneys on staff are ineligible for the program. Therefore, one of the very first things we do is check the attorney count of every applicant. Those with fewer than 3 on staff are immediately declined. We spend virtually no time evaluating them. Hence, our team is freed up to perform a careful analysis of firms that do meet the baseline criteria of having 3 or more attorneys on staff.

It's important to note that passing the triage does not guarantee that we will make a bet on that particular company. We don't choose to cover every law firm with 3 or more attorneys on staff. Triage is just the first step. When a company passes the initial triage, it means we're going to invest our time in giving them a closer look. That's it.

Do you realize that triage is also a tool you can use when it comes to the Bible?

This may surprise you, but there are over 10,000 religions on the planet today. Ten thousand! With such a vast pool of choices, many people freeze and choose to commit to no holy book at all. Others scramble and choose to accept every sacred book. In other words, they consider all sacred texts to be equally valid. In this line of thinking, religion simply reflects your personal preference— "your truth" instead of the truth.

But there's a problem. When holy books make conflicting claims, they can't all be true. Logically, they could all be false, but conflicting claims cannot all be true. In other words, if the Bible is true, then any claim that conflicts with what it says is false. So, with all of these books making conflicting claims, how does someone choose to believe the Bible instead of the Quran, or the Book of Mormon, or the Dao de Jing, or the Hindu Vedas, or any of the other innumerable sacred writings out there? How do we know which ones to study or where to even start?

As someone who specializes in selecting "winners" out of vast pools of applicants, I strongly suggest you triage. That is unless you're prepared to dedicate your life to intense study of the holy books of 10,000+ religions. I say 'intense' because if you hustle to master one world religion per week, you'll be able to study all of them in a cool 192 years or so. So, you'd better get to work! And please allow me to highlight a few gems you can look forward to exploring:[1]

• *Pastafarianism*- a supernatural flying spaghetti monster created the world while drunk ~5,000 years ago.
• *Presleyterianism*- worships Elvis Presley. Followers must look toward Las Vegas once per day and follow command-ments involving products Elvis enjoyed—including Pepsi and El Producto cigars.
• *Jediism*- a religion based on the Star Wars movies, with its god being manifest as "the force".

These are evidently, actual religions with actual people who practice them. Though these examples may seem out-landish (they are), they serve to highlight the point. With a finite amount of time on this planet, it makes no sense to aimlessly survey every holy book under the sun. You can efficiently determine which book(s) deserve an in-depth evaluation with a proper triage. By quickly disposing of those that don't meet the criteria, you can focus your energy on holy books that have given humanity a compelling reason to believe they're true. For instance, if there were, say, a reliable historical event that proved someone had risen from the dead, we'd want to investigate what that person had to say on the matter. Let's dial in our focus together...

---

1. https://safe365.com/

Chapter Two

THE ULTIMATE SUBJECT MATTER EXPERT

Insurance companies regularly engage expert witnesses to help defend the people and companies they insure. These subject matter experts are people who have particular knowledge or experience beyond what an average layperson would have. In my business, we utilize experts to help establish whether a professional's actions fall below the standard of care they owe to their clients. The experts help us understand if the person we're covering is actually at fault or not.

As scientifically and technologically advanced as modern expert witness testimony can be, this isn't a new concept. Over 2,000 years ago, the Roman Empire used midwives, handwriting specialists, and land surveyors as experts in court cases. Getting testimony from specially trained or educated people in a particular field is a tried-and-true practice. It's just common sense.

When it comes down to it, subject matter experts help laypeople understand complex and nuanced information. For this reason, when we're dealing with the source of all

THE ULTIMATE SUBJECT MATTER EXPERT 9

complex and nuanced information, it'd be wise to consult the ultimate subject matter expert—someone with a supreme, particular, specialized knowledge of all things to do with God.

We know just the guy, don't we?

His name is Jesus Christ!

Another book in this series explains in-depth how we know Jesus is who He said He is - the Son of God. It would be outside of the scope of this book to restate it all here, but please allow me to provide a brief high-level overview of the rationale:

In short, unlike other religions, Christianity hinges upon an actual historical event. The bottom line is, if Jesus rose from the dead, Christianity is true. We can study it from many different angles, but the fact is, either the resurrection happened, or it didn't. In *Jesus: Fib, Dead, or God?,* we evaluate the F.A.C.T.S. The term F.A.C.T.S. refers to several historical facts that are so well attested that they are accepted as absolutely true by virtually all specialist scholars. That means not only Christian scholars, but liberal scholars, and even atheist scholars accept them as true. When we examine this set of undeniable universally accepted facts, the only logical conclusion is that Jesus did, indeed rise from the dead. Therefore, I don't believe Jesus was a liar. I believe Jesus is who He said He is, the Son of God.

Now, call me crazy, but it's a personal policy of mine to listen to people who:

• **Claim to be the Son of God** – "'Very truly I tell you', Jesus answered, 'before Abraham was born, I am!'" [1]

• **Perform Miracles** – "Jesus stretched out His hand and touched him, saying, 'I am willing; be cleansed.' And immediately his leprosy was cleansed." [2]

• **Predict they'll be killed and rise again in 3 days** – "Jesus answered and said to them, 'Destroy this temple, and in three days I will raise it up.'" [3]

• **...Actually die and rise again in 3 days, proving they are indeed the Son of God** – "But the angel answered and said to the women, 'Do not be afraid, for I know that you are looking for Jesus who was crucified. He is not here; he has risen, just as he said.'" [4]

This isn't a new revelation. Listening to the ultimate subject matter expert has been sound advice for nearly 2,000 years. You're probably familiar with this event that underscores the point:

> *"On the third day, there was a wedding at Cana of Galilee, and the mother of Jesus was there; and both Jesus and his disciples were invited to the wedding. When the wine was all gone, the mother of Jesus said to him, 'They have no more wine.' Jesus said to her, '[Dear] woman, what is that to you and to me? My time [to act and be revealed] has not yet come.' His mother said to the servants, 'Whatever He says to you, do it.' Now there were six stone waterpots*

---

1. John 8:48

2. Matthew 8:3

3. John 2:19

4. Matthew 28:5-6

set there for the Jewish custom of purification (cere-monial washing), containing twenty or thirty gallons each. Jesus said to the servants, 'Fill the waterpots with water.' So they filled them up to the brim. Then He said to them, 'Draw some out now and take it to the headwaiter [of the banquet].' And when the headwaiter tasted the water which had been turned into wine, not knowing where it came from (though the servants who had drawn the water knew) he called to the bridegroom, and said to him, 'Everyone else serves his best wine first, and when people have drunk freely, then he serves that which is not so good, but you have kept back the good wine until now.' [5]

This well-known passage is the first recorded miracle per-formed by Jesus during his earthly ministry. It's amazing on so many levels, not least of which is the wisdom we see from Mary, the mother of Jesus. "*Whatever He says to you, do it.*" Is that not the most pragmatic advice imaginable? No details, no qualifiers, no caveats–He's the Son of God–just do it.

It seems obvious now, doesn't it? Here's a way we can triage the holy writings of 10,000+ religions on the planet:

Prioritize the book(s) endorsed by the Son of God.

In other words, whatever He says to you, do it!

Well, here is what He says to you. Jesus taught that the holy scriptures of the Bible are:

---

5. John 2:1-11

- **Inerrant (cannot be mistaken) -** *"You are mistaken, not knowing the Scriptures, nor the power of God."*[6]
- **Inspired by the Holy Spirit**- *"But the Helper, the Holy Spirit, whom the Father will send in My name, He will teach you all things, and bring to your remembrance all things that I said to you."*[7]
- **Timeless**- *"It is easier for heaven and earth to pass away than for one stroke of a letter of God's Law to fail and become void."*[8]
- **Historically accurate**- *"And as it was in the days of Noah, so will it be in the days of the Son of Man: They ate, they drank, they married wives, they were given in marriage, until the day that Noah entered the ark, and the flood came and destroyed them all."*[9]

And if that's not enough, how's this for an endorsement:

> *"Then Jesus was led by the Spirit into the wilderness to be tempted by the devil. After fasting forty days and forty nights, he was hungry. The tempter (Satan) came to him and said, 'If you are the Son of God, tell these stones to become bread.' Jesus answered, 'It is written: 'Man shall not live on bread alone, but on every word that comes from the mouth of God.'"* [10]

---

6. Matthew 22:29

7. John 14:26

8. Luke 16:17

9. Matthew 24:37-39

10. Matthew 4:1-4

When Jesus is tempted by the devil, he rejects the enemy by quoting the.... ~~Quran~~, the... ~~Book of Mormon~~, the... ~~sacred texts of Confucianism~~, the... ~~Buddhist Tripitaka~~, the... ~~Hindu Vedas~~, **THE BIBLE**. When Jesus states, "it is written," it means He's quoting Old Testament scripture. His use of "It is written" essentially means, "God says." In other words, Jesus is saying that what the Bible says *is* what God says. Let's also take a look at this particular scripture He used in the passage: "*Man shall not live on bread alone, but on every word that comes from the mouth of God.*"

Wow.

Jesus Christ states that the Bible is literally more important than physical sustenance. He modeled the use of the Bible in everyday life and referred to the scriptures constantly. By all accounts, He taught us that the Bible is the authoritative Word of God. With this in mind, it's time we got to work...

Chapter Three

THE PROCESS

Let's restate our baseline challenge: there are over 10,000 religions on the planet. These religions have innumerable "sacred" texts associated with them. These texts can't all be true because they make conflicting claims. So, how do we determine which of these, if any, are true?

The purpose of the triage is to prioritize the holy book(s) that give us the greatest chance of success. Therefore, our eligibility requirement is based on Jesus. Who would be more qualified to advise us on the matter than the Son of God Himself? Now, watch what happens when we apply what we've discussed to this point:

Eligibility Requirement:

The holy book(s) must be endorsed by the Son of the living God.

Applicants:

1. *The Bible*: **PASS**. Jesus taught that the Bible is the authoritative word of God and is more important than

physical sustenance.

2. *Literally every other holy book in existence*: **FAIL**. Not endorsed by Jesus. Directly contradicted by Jesus because He stated that "no one comes to the Father except through Me."

Friend- our rationale for belief in the Bible isn't an enigma. Stated plainly: I choose to believe Jesus rose from the dead due to F.A.C.T.S. Therefore, He is exactly who He said He is; the Son of God. Since He's the Son of God, my view of the Bible is based on what HE taught about it. Jesus taught that the Bible is the authoritative word of God.

Boom! "God said it, I believe it that settles it, right?" Listen, I love that sentiment, and I agree with it, but I would challenge you to go even further. I believe there are several compelling reasons that every Christian should dig deeper on why we believe the Bible:

1. **The stakes genuinely can't get any higher** – as believers, we're staking our eternity that the Bible is true. Naturally, with so much on the line, it's not something we ought to decide haphazardly or on a whim.

2. **We're called to share the Good News in a skeptical world** - every Christian has a direct command from Jesus to share the gospel and make disciples. Knowing *that* the Bible is true is an awesome start. However, explaining *why* you believe the Bible is true is a much more powerful testimony to share with unbelievers. Think of it like this: let's say you were boarding a flight that was about to take off in bad weather. Perhaps you read that planes all around the world get struck by lightning almost daily (they do). How would you feel if the pilot told you he knows that

lightning strikes aren't a major concern, but he's not exactly sure why? Personally, I may be happy that he believes it's not a problem, but I'd sure feel a whole lot better if he could explain why he believes it's not a problem.

3. **Spiritual Development**- In *The Purpose Driven Life*, Rick Warren explained that "God's ultimate goal for your life on earth is not comfort, but character development. He wants you to grow up spiritually and become like Christ. Becoming like Christ does not mean losing your personality or becoming a mindless clone. God created your uniqueness, so he doesn't want to destroy it. Christlikeness is all about transforming your character, not your personality."

4. **Relationship Building**- Jesus said that the greatest commandment is to *"love the Lord your God with all your heart, with all your soul, and with all your mind."* So, we're supposed to use our minds to study the ways of God and enter deeper into a relationship with Him.

Digging deeper is right in line with where we are in our evaluation process. From an insurance perspective, the triage is never the end-all-be-all; it's just the beginning. It's a critical first step, but it carries with it a very low level of commitment. Remember, we're simply prioritizing the accounts that we think give us the best chance to succeed. So, we haven't actually committed to covering anybody at this stage. In other words, passing the triage plus two dollars will get you a cup of coffee.

What follows the initial triage is a thorough underwriting of our remaining potential "winners". It's here that we give them a much closer look. And this next step is not a "nice to have." It's imperative. Suppose I had gone all-in and covered every company that passed my initial triage. In that case, I'd have lost huge sums of my employers' money and been out of the business long ago.

Our underwriting process involves examining specific characteristics of the company seeking coverage. We have a particular risk "appetite" that dictates what we're looking for. Among other things, we look at where the company is located, how long they've been in business, how much revenue they generate each year, the experience level of their staff, what type of services they perform, what types of projects they're involved in, who their clients are, whether they've been sued before, if they've ever had licensure or disciplinary issues in the past, etc. We laser in on these risk characteristics individually, and then pull back and use them to get a picture of the company as a whole.

That's where we're headed with the Bible. We're going to take a closer look at some specific characteristics and then pull back and assess what we see. With the triage complete, it's time for us to crank up the heat on our evaluation. Let's go...

UNDERWRITING

UNDERWRITING

I'd like you to think about a place that's about 10-minute drive from your home. Assuming an average speed of 30 miles per hour, that destination would be approximately 5 miles away. Do you have your place in mind? Alright. Now, if you stood in your front yard and yelled at the top of your lungs, do you think anyone would be able to hear you at that place? Of course not. But do you know what they *would* be able to hear? A lion's roar. It's actually hard to fathom just how powerful that is. Five miles away![1]

Of course, that's just one of the many reasons that lions are referred to as the "king of the jungle." Lions are one of the most widely recognized animal symbols known to man. We see them everywhere from sculptures and paintings to national flags and sports teams.

These animals don't have an easy life. At 2-3 years old, young male lions get kicked out of their pride and must attempt to take over another male's pride.[2] This usually

1. https://naturenoon.com/

2. National Geographic

involves a fight to the death, with only about 1 in 8 male lions surviving to adulthood.

Lions are considered apex predators. That's to say that they are at the top of their food chain and have no natural predators. While lions average 250-500 lbs., they hunt preys that run 400-1,200 lbs. – wildebeest, zebra, giraffe, and buffalo to name a few. Lions can reach speeds of up to 50 miles per hour and can jump nearly 40 feet. They have a bite force of 650 pounds per square inch. And they consume 10-15 pounds of meat per day. [3]

I share this information with you to make one thing absolutely clear –

The last thing on Earth that a lion needs is protection from me.

I took a handful of years of Karate classes growing up and might well have been the least dangerous person who ever set foot in that dojo.

Likewise, the last thing on Earth that the Bible needs is a defense from me or anyone else for that matter. It was Charles Spurgeon who famously said, "The Word of God is like a lion. You don't have to defend a lion. All you have to do is let the lion loose, and the lion will defend itself."

As we move on to underwrite the Bible, I'll do my best to let the lion loose, stay out of the way, and simply point to what I see. Let's go.

---

3. https://www.fieldandstream.com/

Chapter Four

COLLECTION

C harles Ponzi is among the most infamous con artists in history. The term "Ponzi Scheme" remains a common expression today; roughly a century after it was coined. This phrase refers to Ponzi's "too good to be true" money-making scheme, where he guaranteed investors a 100% return on their money within 90 days. His purported strategy involved purchasing discounted stamps in foreign countries and re-deeming them at full price in the United States. In reality, Ponzi was using the money from new investors to pay off the funds promised to earlier investors. By the time he was caught, Ponzi had swindled his investors out of roughly $20 million dollars, equivalent to over $250 million dollars today.

Ouch.

Ponzi served 14 years in prison for his scheme.

Infamous as it may be, the scope of Ponzi's namesake scheme pales in comparison to Bernie Madoff's investment scandal. Madoff was, at one time, among the most respected names on Wall Street. That was until his "one big lie" came to light. Madoff ran the largest Ponzi scheme in history, defrauding investors out of over $65 billion dollars. His oper-ation had all of the classic characteristics of a Ponzi scheme:
  • Investors are lured in by the promise of exceptional

returns with virtually no downside risk.

- Investors are convinced that they are part of an ex-clusive club of sorts.

- The purported investment strategy is highly secretive and highly complex.

- In reality, the con artist is simply using the money from new investors to pay off earlier investors.

- The con artist gets very rich in the process.

- A constant stream of new investors is needed to con-tinue the scheme.

- The fraud is discovered when the required stream of new investors eventually dries up.

- The "central operator" trades their super-extravagant lifestyle for a lengthy prison sentence.

The "central operator" of a Ponzi scheme is the con artist; the brains behind it. Charles Ponzi and Bernie Madoff are two of the best-known operators, but there are plenty of others:[1]

- Lou Perlman, the creator of the boy bands N'Sync and Backstreet boys—stole $300 million from investors using faux companies that only existed on paper.

- Reed Slatkin, a tech entrepreneur—stole $593 million from investors and funneled it into the Church of Scientology cult.

---

1. https://www.cnn.com/

- Scott Rothstein, an attorney—stole $1.2 billion by getting investors to buy into fraudulent legal settlements.

- R Allen Stanford, a financier—stole $7 billion over the course of 20 years, using fake certificates of deposit.

While the particulars of each fraud vary, they all revolve around an individual con artist. The individual purports to have special (secretive) information to deliver the extraordinary return on investment. Fundamentally, it's one individual making a claim.

Do you know what that sounds very similar to? Many of the holy books in existence. Many involve one individual who; (1) claims to have heard some special revelation from God, (2) writes it down, and (3) convinces others they should listen to him.

As a trained evaluator of risk, this catches my eye. While we can't predict the future, we can certainly look back at trends from the past to help make better decisions as we advance. Therefore, as we dive into the specific characteristics of the Bible, we must recognize a critical distinction.

The Bible is different than many other holy books because it's not actually a book; it's a collection of books - sixty-six of them, to be specific.
2

The sixty-six books were written by over 40 authors, most of whom never met one another. These authors hail from a myriad of backgrounds - kings, generals, tax collectors, fishermen, missionaries, doctors, historians, and more. They wrote these books in three different languages – Hebrew,

Greek, and Aramaic – and on three different continents – Asia, Africa, and Europe. The books cover hundreds of topics, and the writing occurred over the course of 1,500 years.

Let's put this in perspective. One hundred and fifty years ago, it was 1872. At that time in America:[3]

- Slavery had been outlawed for less than a decade.

- Most children got their education in one-room schoolhouses.

- The horse and buggy was a popular mode of transportation

- Tooth brushing was not a common practice.

- Doing laundry involved making homemade soap, followed by manual soaking, rubbing, rinsing, and ironing each garment.

Yikes! Does this sound like an obscure world to you? It sure does to me, and that was only 150 years ago. The period over which the Bible was written was ten times as long! So, for those of you keeping score at home, we have a math problem to solve:

Sixty-six books + Forty authors from a myriad of backgrounds, most of whom never met one another + Three languages + Three continents + Hundreds of topics + Fifteen hundred years = One.

Yes, one. As in one cohesive story. Miraculous as it may seem (it is), these sixty-six books come together to tell one

---

unified story about the redemption of humanity. In other words, the Bible is basically the polar opposite of having just one guy who claims to have special (secretive) information from God. Let's note this first characteristic on our risk evaluation and move on. We're just getting started...

Risk Characteristics:

1. **C**ollection

Chapter Five

SCIENCE

Is the Bible scientifically accurate? For centuries, unbelievers have been relentless in their pursuit to prove that it isn't. One of them being Charles Darwin's *Theory of Evolution*—192 years ago. Atheists breathlessly crowned Darwin their champion in a manufactured "war between science and religion." Today, Darwin's theory has been eviscerated by advances in science and technology. The so-called "war between science and religion" continues to be unveiled for what it truly is - a war in philosophy. In other words, it's not science versus religion – it's good science versus bad science. Believers point to science as a means to understand the universe that God created. Unbelievers treat science as a religion unto itself.

So how does all these factor into our evaluation of the Bible? In short, unbelievers don't want the Bible to be true. Therefore, science is just one of the many strategies used in an effort to discredit the Bible. If they can prove it's inaccurate on scientific matters, then it can't be trusted on spiritual issues either. With this in mind, we must face this issue head-on.

Pastor John MacArthur made a point in a recent sermon on this topic that hit me like a ton of bricks.[1] It's simple and obvious, yet profound. Here it is: Whoever created the universe understands it perfectly. Of course, the designer of the universe would be a supreme expert on how it works.

I'm very familiar with this issue of expertise as a professional evaluator of risk. When a company claims to have expertise in a particular field, our underwriting process involves a review of evidence to support or refute their claim. Here's an example; when a law firm applies for coverage, I generally always review their website. The website is a place the firm advertises its various services and areas of expertise.

Occasionally, I'd come across a law firm whose website indicated they were experts in all sorts of areas of the law. It included specialized practice areas like medical malpractice litigation. However, when I reviewed their application for coverage, they reported that 100% of the cases they actually handled were something different, like criminal defense matters such as DUI's. There was a huge disconnection between the firm's claims of expertise and the reality of their practice.

So, let's apply this to the matter at hand. The Bible claims that God designed the universe and everything inside of it. Therefore, as the designer, He has supreme expertise on how the universe works.

But how could we test the validity of that claim of expertise? Well, the Bible also claims that God fully inspired the

---

1. John MacArthur

human writers and is the author of the scriptures.[2] Therefore, these two claims together look like this:

The author of the Bible is the ultimate expert on how the universe works. Are you with me? The implications are fascinating. If these claims are true, the author of the Bible would not need to wait around for scientific discovery to know how it works. If it's true, the Bible wouldn't just be scientifically accurate, friend. We should actually find evidence within the text that indicates the author is out in front of science! Here's what I mean:

1. **DNA** – On February 28, 1953, physicist Francis Crick interrupted lunch at The Eagle Pub in Cambridge, England, to announce that he and American biologist, James Watson had "discovered the secret of life." [3] Indeed, our understanding of the organic world would never be the same. They had discovered DNA.

But wait a minute. Hadn't the "secret of life" been ironed out by Darwin's theory of evolution a century earlier?

Today, we know that Darwin's theory was wrong. The idea that matter, energy, and random chance could produce our world is now a relic of the past. Likewise, the idea that more complex living organisms blindly "evolved" from simpler ones has not and cannot be proven. We can boil down this failure to one word; information.

There is a level of complexity within every cell that Darwin and his generation never dreamed of. Specifically, there is a

---

2. 2 Timothy 3:16

3. www.bbc.com

complex coded information system within every cell. It can communicate within itself and pass information around. In fact, the entire organic world is like a book packed with highly sophisticated, complex biological information.

A world that is literally built on information systems is a massive problem for atheists. It's been scientifically proven that matter can only hold information; it can't produce it. Information only comes from one place...intelligence.

Said differently, messages only come from one place; the minds. Matter cannot create a code system such as a language, yet the chemicals of DNA literally make up a genetic alphabet. This is why DNA is referred to as the "instruction book of life". This genetic alphabet encodes instructions for building and replicating all things. And this language is unimaginably complex. For example, the instructions written in this genetic alphabet for a "simple" single-celled amoeba are the equivalent of the amount of information in 1,000 encyclopedias. And that's a single cell. If laid out end to end, the DNA code within every person would go to the sun and back numerous times.

The bottom line is, prior to this discovery in the 1950's, it was widely believed that matter, energy, and blind chance were all that was needed for "evolution." Information was omitted. The discovery that everything in the universe is encoded in DNA is a discovery that God has spoken. In other words, He dictated the "instruction book of life."

Scientifically, this was discovered about 70 years ago. But where else have I heard that before? Ah yes, in **the very first chapter in the very first book of the Bible!**

- And God said, "Let there be light."

- And God said, "Let there be a vault between the waters to separate water from water."

- And God said, "Let the water under the sky be gathered to one place, and let dry ground appear."

- And God said, "Let the land produce vegetation."

- And God said, "Let there be lights in the vault of the sky to separate the day from the night."

- And God said, "Let the water teem with living creatures, and let birds fly above the earth across the vault of the sky."

- And God said, "Let the land produce living creatures according to their kinds..."

- Then God said, "Let us make mankind in our image, in our likeness..."

The author of the Bible reported that the "instruction book of life" had been spoken into existence about 3,000 years before scientific discovery did. But that's not the only area where we've seen this phenomenon.

2. Hydrology – Scientific breakthroughs in the 17th century gave us an understanding of the Earth's waters. Before this, it was believed there were subterranean reservoirs. We now know that it's the same mass of water that cycles around. The world hasn't gained any or lost any. As for the author of the Bible, He wrote about this hydrological cycle in the Book of Job, 2,300 years earlier. "He wraps up the waters in his clouds, yet the clouds do not burst under their weight.... He draws up the drops of water, which distill as rain to the streams; the clouds pour down their moisture and abundant showers fall on mankind... Have you entered the storehouses of the snow or seen the storehouses of the hail?"[4]

3. Astronomy – Before the telescope was invented in the 17th century, lead scientists estimated that the sky contained between 1,022 and 1,055 stars. Today, we know that there are 100 billion of them in our galaxy alone. This apparently would not come as a surprise to the author of the Bible. About 2,300 years before the discovery of the telescope, the author wrote in the book of Jeremiah that the stars cannot be counted, nor the heavens measured. [5]

4. Meteorology- In 1643, mathematician Evangelista Torricelli discovered that air has weight. A few thousand years earlier, the author of the Bible wrote about the "weight of the wind". [6]

5. Geology- In 1851, Leon Foucault demonstrated that the Earth rotates. The author of the Bible wrote about the Earth being "turned like a clay to the seal" about 2,500 years earlier. At that time, a device similar to a rolling pin was rolled across clay to stamp your signature. That is, the author of the Bible described the Earth as rotating on an axis thousands of years before it was discovered scientifically.

6. Physiology- if someone was sick during medieval times, a popular medical treatment was to bleed the patient out. In fact, blood-letting was used as a medical procedure as late as the 1920's. Meanwhile, the author of the Bible wrote

---

4. Job 26, 36, 38

5. Jeremiah 33:22

6. Job 28:25

that "the life of a creature is in the blood" nearly 3,500 years earlier.

If the Bible is the truth, it is the ultimate standard of truth. That's not an "anti-science" position. Instead, it's a position that puts science in its proper place – as a means to further discover the universe that God created. We may be well served to trade "I believe in science" for "I believe in the Lord Jesus Christ."

Today, a popular catchphrase in our society is to "follow the science." But, interestingly, we've found that as science progresses, we can trace it right to Bible scriptures that were written thousands of years earlier. By all accounts, it appears that the author of the Bible precedes scientific discovery. So let's add it to our list and move on...

Risk Characteristics:

1. **C**ollection

2. **O**ut in front of science

Chapter Six

RESILIENT

"Let me get this straight. You guys *want* to cover companies that have been sued?"

They did their best to be polite, but my new co-workers couldn't help but stare at us as if we each had three heads. My team and I were being introduced as new hires at a very large, name-brand insurance company. As we explained our underwriting appetite, it became clear that our approach was completely foreign to most in the crowd. As a large, established insurance company, their general approach was to cover as many low-risk companies as possible. They would cover such a staggering volume of low-risk companies so they could pay the cost of the few that did have claims and still make a handsome profit.

A critical component of this strategy is setting parameters to ensure that the companies you're covering are low risk. For instance, a company that had been sued would be deemed ineligible (high-risk), and declined coverage. Imagine the looks on their faces as we explained that the only companies we would even consider covering were those that had been sued in the past.

As previously discussed, our specialty underwriting brand is designed to find "diamonds in the rough" amongst thousands of applicants. And if employed correctly, this strategy could be highly effective. The reasoning could be a book unto itself. Still, one of the important factors is that the companies we cover have been tested. By definition, virtually every applicant we consider has been attacked in the form of a lawsuit. This concept of demonstrated resilience is a risk factor we look at closely. We can learn a lot about a company when they've been tested. I'd much prefer to bet on a company that's been established for decades and been through some lawsuits than a brand-new start-up company with no track record.

The Bible tells us to celebrate when we get tested. *"Consider it pure joy, my brothers and sisters, whenever you face trials of many kinds, because you know that the testing of your faith produces perseverance. Let perseverance finish its work so that you may be mature and complete, not lacking anything."*[1]

Indeed. We know that testing produces perseverance in all sorts of facets of life. When I first began playing the guitar, my fingertips were so sore that it hurt even to touch the strings. But eventually, they toughened up and got calloused, so playing wasn't painful at all. Likewise, if we test our muscles with exercise and weightlifting, they come back stronger. And how about this one? Can you picture doing your day job in front of 25,000 people who are screaming at you, cursing you, and wanting nothing more than for you to fail? I'm always amazed when a professional athlete does their job in the midst of these conditions. I can picture a pro basketball player calmly standing at the free-throw line as boos rain out, fans stomp their feet and wave their hands, and the pressure mounts. So often, the player appears as if they're

---

1. James 1:2

by themselves in the gym. They calmly take the ball, breathe, and score the free throw. How could that be?

They've been tested.

Now, we all know that testing is not divvied up equally amongst everyone. For instance, the home team fans surely boo the visiting team's star player much more than they do the third-string reserve player or the equipment manager. And that shows that if those less tested individuals had to stand up and shoot with the fans cursing them, their chances will be comparatively low since they haven't been tested in that area.

Let's apply this to the matter at hand. In short, there isn't a book or collection of books on the planet that has received the testing that the Bible has and continues to receive. There have been efforts to undermine the word of God quite literally since the dawn of humanity. The first attack came when Satan tempted Eve, *"Did God really say that you must not eat from any tree in the garden?"*[2] He undermined the trustworthiness of God's word. Since then, there's been more of the same from an unending litany of scholars, critics, false teachers, cultists, and complainers. People spend their entire careers and lives in pursuit of disproving the Bible. And that's in places where it's legal. The Bible is also banned in 52 countries. There are maps to categorize countries where Bibles are; (1) difficult/dangerous to obtain, (2) illegal or highly restricted, or (3) strictly illegal and only available through covert smuggling. [3]

---

2. Genesis 3:1

3. Persecution.com

That said, we need not travel to distant lands or rub elbows with disgruntled atheist professors to encounter testing of the Bible. As Pastor Voddie Bauchum puts it, "there are those who read the Bible like a judge, trying to find something wrong, working hard to find something wrong with it."[4] When it comes to this particular type of testing, I can't help but think of Joan Calamezzo. Joan is a character from one of my favorite sitcoms, *Parks and Rec*. She hosts a local talk show and introduces herself as "legendary newswoman, Joan Calamezzo." Her trademark is "Gotcha Journalism", complete with a "Joan Gotcha" theme song and scantily clad dancers. Joan makes it her goal to find the most negative possible aspects of any story and is outwardly disappointed when a purported scandal is disproven. While on assignment, Joan makes sure her cameraman sets the scene she desires. "Let's go ahead and get some shots of chipped paint and crying babies. How about some of those spooky traffic lights? You know the drill." Exaggerated as her features may be, I can't help but see the parallels with this particular style of testing that the Bible is subjected to around the world daily.

In the next section, we'll dig deeper into some specific objections to the Bible. First, however, suppose there were a series of inconsistencies, errors, or contradictions that could falsify the Bible. In that case, we know it would have been accomplished long, long ago. Brilliant minds have worked doggedly for generations to disprove the Bible, yet it remains standing. It's nothing, if not resilient in the face of testing. So let's add it to our notes and move on...

Risk Characteristics:

---

4. Voddie Bauchum- Why I Choose to Believe the Bible-YouTube

1. **C**ollection

2. **O**ut in front of science

3. **R**esilient

4. **R**evered

***

Chapter Seven

REVERED

I hate shopping, but I love my wife, so I found myself in a Costco Wholesale store one night after work a couple of weeks ago. For better or worse, the store is located directly on the way home from my office. I was there on official Parent Teacher Organization business—sent to pick up supplies for a winter festival organized by my wife at the kids' school.

My game plan was simple: get in, get the items on the list, and get out. No messing around. Unfortunately, the execution of said plan was something far from stellar. I pictured myself methodically securing each item like some sort of highly trained special ops agent. In reality, I looked more like Moses with a shopping cart - aimlessly wandering around the desert for 40 years.

Notwithstanding my ignorance of the Costco Store layout, I eventually got everything on the list, and then some. As I meandered toward the back of the store, a flash of purple caught my attention.

It was Raisin Bran. But not your typical grocery store box of Raisin Bran. This was an industrial-sized Costco box containing two monster bags of cereal within it instead of just one.

Jackpot.

I was hungry and still about 20 minutes away from home. That box was in my cart without even breaking stride.

Somewhere out there, a marketing person is smiling. Their product was in the right place at the right time, triggering an unplanned purchase. Product positioning is a fascinating thing. There's a science and psychology to it. Companies invest massive amounts of resources to study it, and they sure aren't doing that because it's costing them money. Believe it or not, the average American consumer spends over $5,000 a year on impulse purchases. The number one type of impulse buy? You guessed it: food. It's no wonder grocery stores position complementary products like chips and salsa together. Likewise, cash registers are typically surrounded by candy, gum, mints, and other trinkets.

When it comes to visual marketing, retailers utilize a ranking system for shelf space. Anything below 3 feet high is considered to be in the least desirable "stoop level." This is because shoppers don't like to bend down and rarely browse in this area. In fact, had that cereal been tucked away in the bottom corner of the display, I probably wouldn't have even noticed it. Above stoop level, we find "touch level," which is 3-4 feet high. This level mainly contains products aimed at kids. But the prime real estate, the most desirable placements on the shelf, are located at "eye level." This level runs 4-5 feet high and is the area that receives by far the most attention from browsers. Hence the phrase, "Eye Level is Buy Level."

This principle isn't limited to retail stores. Consider the newspaper business. Traditionally, only the top half of the front page of a newspaper can be seen when it's displayed. Therefore, the day's biggest news is placed "above the fold" in the prime position. That's not to say that the other stories are unimportant. Still, an organization is going to place what is most important to them front and center.

That includes the church.

They go by various names, but almost every Christian Church has a public statement of beliefs. These statements affirm what the church teaches.

As I began to explore various statements of belief of respected Christian churches and ministry organizations, a trend began to jump off the page. Here are the opening lines of each organizations' respective statement of belief:

The Bible is inspired; the only authoritative word of God. -Victory Church, Middlefield, CT. Pastor Peter Leal, Sr.

We teach that the Bible is God's written revelation to man, and thus the 66 books of the Bible given to us by the Holy Spirit constitute the plenary (inspired equally in all parts) Word of God. -Grace Community Church, Sun Valley, CA. Pastor John MacArthur.

We believe that the Bible is the Word of God, fully inspired and without error in the original manuscripts, written under the inspiration of the Holy Spirit, and that it has supreme authority in all matters of faith and conduct. -Bethlehem Baptist Church, Minneapolis, MN. Pastor John Piper.

The Bible is God's Word to all people. It was written by human authors under the supernatural guidance of the Holy Spirit. Because it was inspired by God, the Bible is truth without any mixture of error and is completely relevant to our daily lives. -Elevation Church, Charlotte, NC. Pastor Steven Furtick.

We believe that the Holy Bible was written by men divinely inspired, and is a perfect treasure of heavenly instruction, that it has God for its author, salvation for its end, and truth without any mixture of error for its matter; that it reveals the principles by which God will judge us; and therefore is, and shall remain to the end of the world, the true center of Christian union, and the supreme standard by which all human conduct, creeds, and opinions should be tried. -HeartCry Missionary Society (Pastor Paul Washer), Radford, VA.

We believe the Bible to be the inspired, the only infallible, authoritative Word of God revealing the love of God to the world. -Billy Graham Evangelistic Association, Charlotte, NC.

The Holy Scripture is the only sufficient, certain, and infallible rule of all saving knowledge, faith, and obedience. -Voddie Baucham Ministries, Spring, TX.

Wow. The authority of the Bible is positioned "above the fold" in every case. As a risk evaluator, this catches my eye.

I'm conditioned to look for stability and consistency because I know what often happens when there's a lack of it present. If there is one thing that causes my ears to perk up and detect an increased risk of a company being sued, it's change. Mistakes often happen during transition periods, especially when the change is drastic. For example, we prefer to cover companies with moderate and steady growth over time. Slow, continued growth may sound boring on the surface. Still, it's much more attractive to cover than a company that anticipates they'll triple their sales in the coming year. The same goes for staff count. Rapid hiring or, in the other direction, layoffs, are an indicator of risk. Finally, events like mergers, acquisitions, and changes in senior leadership are all things that we'd need to give a hard look—consistency matters.

If orthodox Christ-followers had a drastically different view of the Bible than Christ Himself, it would certainly give me pause. But this "above the fold" consistency puts that issue to rest. It's been nearly 2,000 years since Jesus Christ claimed that the Bible is more important than physical sustenance. The fact that His followers (the church) still revere the Bible today is a trend I'm very pleased to see. Let's add it to our notes.

Chapter Eight

TRUST BUT VERIFY

U nited States President Ronald Reagan and Soviet Union General Secretary Mikhail Gorbachev signed the Intermediate-Range Nuclear Forces (INF) Treaty on 12/08/1987. This treaty served as a disarmament agreement, banning both countries from possessing various intermediate-range and ground-launched missiles. As part of the agreement, existing missiles were destroyed – most were exploded while unarmed or cut in half.

A mutual inspection process was put in place to ensure that both sides complied with the destruction of their existing missiles. Each side could conduct up to 20 short-notice inspections per year, sending observers to monitor the other's elimination efforts as they occurred.[1]

President Reagan's signature phrase regarding the inspections was "Trust but verify." Secretary Gorbachev quipped, "You repeat that at every meeting," to which President Reagan replied, "I like it."[2]

---

1. https://www.armscontrol.org/factsheets/INFtreaty

2. leadergrow.com/articles/trust-but-verify/

As a risk evaluator, I'm no stranger to the "Trust but verify" sentiment. Insurance contracts are built on verified trust. The companies we cover trust in our promise to defend them should they get sued. Similarly, we trust that the companies applying for coverage provide us with accurate information to evaluate.

While this relationship requires trust, it's far from blind faith. For example, our application for coverage requires that the applicant report to us any claims they have filed under their previous insurance policies. This allows us to evaluate their track record. If a company reports that they've never filed a claim on their E&O insurance, we trust them, but we need more. Perhaps their insurance agent also confirms in writing that there have been no claims filed during the period she has represented them. That's even better. We now have multiple consistent accounts from people who would know firsthand whether or not the company had filed previous claims. Still, we take it one step further. We obtain "loss runs" on every company we offer to cover. Loss runs are official reports detailing the claims filed under previous insurance policies. These reports allow us to verify what was previously reported, and can only be generated by the insurance company. Notice how each step in this process builds upon the other. The firsthand account from the applicant company is a great start, multiple accounts (if they're consistent) are even better, and finally, the official report seals the deal. When all of these items line up, our trust is warranted.

Now let's apply this to the matter at hand. The Bible claims to reflect an eyewitness account of the resurrection of Jesus Christ:

> *"For we did not follow cleverly devised stories when we told you about the coming of our Lord Jesus Christ in power, but we were eyewitnesses of His majesty.*

He received honor and glory from God the Father when the voice came to him from the Majestic Glory, saying, 'This is my Son, whom I love; with Him I am well pleased.' We ourselves heard this voice that came from heaven when we were with him on the sacred mountain."[3]

One of Jesus' twelve apostles, Peter, makes that eyewitness claim. These twelve were with Jesus from the time of His baptism through His entire earthly ministry and resurrection. It's a great start, and there's more. Remember, the Bible is not just one guy claiming to have some secret revelation from God that we should listen to. Here is another account:

"That which was from the beginning, which we have heard, which we have seen with our eyes, which we have looked at and our hands have touched – this we proclaim concerning the Word of life. The life appeared; we have seen it and testify to it, and we proclaim to you the eternal life, which was with the Father and has appeared to us. We proclaim to you what we have seen and heard, so that you also may have fellowship with us. And our fellowship is with the Father and with His Son, Jesus Christ. We write this to make our joy complete."[4]

This passage comes from another Apostle, John. He, too, was in Jesus' innermost circle. Therefore, we have multiple direct accounts from eyewitnesses. And there's more:

---

3. 2 Peter 1:16-18

4. 1 John 1: 1-4

"Many have undertaken to draw up an account of the things that have been fulfilled among us, just as they were handed down to us by those who from the first were eyewitnesses and servants of the word. With this in mind, since I myself have carefully investigated everything from the beginning, I too decided to write an orderly account for you, most excellent Theophilus, that you may know the certainty of the things you have been taught." [5]

This passage comes from Luke. Luke was not an eyewitness and didn't claim to be. Rather, he was an ultra-meticulous historian who traced information from multiple eyewitnesses, including Mary, the mother of Jesus). So, we have multiple direct eyewitness accounts from Jesus' closest followers and a historian who compiled an orderly account based on other eyewitness testimony. This is strong direct evidence, and we can go even another step further:

"Now, brothers and sisters, I want to remind you of the gospel I preached to you, which you received and on which you have taken your stand. By this gospel, you are saved, if you hold firmly to the word I preached to you. Otherwise, you have believed in vain. For what I received I passed on to you with first importance: that Christ died for our sins according to the Scriptures, and that he appeared to Cephas (Peter), and then to the Twelve (apostles). After that, he appeared to more than five hundred of the brothers and sisters at the same time, most of whom are still living, though some have fallen asleep (died). Then he appeared to James, then to all the apostles,

5. Luke 1: 1-4

and last of all, he appeared to me also, as to one abnormally born." [6]

This letter from Paul to the church at Corinth demonstrates that the collection of eyewitness accounts about the resurrection of Jesus was written during the lifetimes of other eyewitnesses – hundreds of them. Paul wrote this letter roughly 20 years after the resurrection. Paul is basically reminding them – this is the creed we were teaching right after the resurrection. Here are specific names of people that the risen Jesus appeared to. There are still hundreds of eyewitnesses alive to be questioned if you want to go talk to them.

Paul was laying his cards on the table. Does it make sense that he would do that if there weren't actually hundreds of eyewitnesses available to ask? I don't believe so.

In summary, we have:

- Direct evidence in the form of multiple eyewitness accounts from Apostles

- An orderly account composed by a meticulous historian who traced information from other eyewitnesses

- Proof that these eyewitness accounts were written during the lifetimes of other eyewitnesses, who could have disputed the story if it weren't true.

Trust but verify. The Bible is indeed an eyewitness document. Let's add it to our notes and move on.

Risk Characteristics:

---

6. 1 Corinthians 15: 1-8

1. **C**ollection

2. **O**ut in front of science

3. **R**esilient

4. **R**evered

5. **E**yewitness

Chapter Nine

CORROBORATED

L et's talk about indirect evidence. As a case study, we'll look at a small law firm that applied for coverage from my company. This particular firm ended up on my desk for review because a former client of theirs had sued them for $250,000. The matter followed a very typical fact pattern:

- The law firm is a plaintiff's personal injury firm.

- Their client was involved in a serious car accident.

- The client was not at fault for the accident.

- The client hired the law firm to sue the responsible party for damages.

- The law firm accepted the case and prepared a lawsuit.

- When the firm filed the suit, it was discovered that they had missed the deadline in which to sue.

- This deadline is called the *statute of limitations*.

- Because the firm did not file the suit within the allotted statute of limitations, the case was dismissed, and the client received nothing.

- The client then sued the law firm for breaching their professional duties.

- The allegation was essentially, "If not for your negligence, I would have been entitled to X dollars."

- The law firm's malpractice carrier settled the case for $250,000.

- The law firm's practice carrier non-renewed their policy due to the loss.

This is a classic "blown statute" malpractice case. I've underwritten hundreds, if not thousands, of law firms involved in this type of situation. Statutes of limitation are missed for a myriad of reasons. These statutes can be complex – they vary based on what state the accident occurred in, the type of accident, the parties involved in the incident, and much more. They are also sometimes changed by lawmakers. So, for example, the typical statute of limitations may be two years in a particular state. However, suppose it turns out that the person being sued was a federal employee who was on the job when they caused the accident. Then, a different time period may apply. Or if the accident occurred across state lines, another time period may apply, and so forth.

Because of this, mistakes happen, even from highly professional and otherwise excellent practitioners. Most insurance companies will (understandably) instantly decline to cover a law firm with a $250,000 loss in their history. My job is to find those "diamonds in the rough" and cover them.

Our challenge here is: did they miss the deadline because they're sloppy? Or was the missed deadline a fluke that is unlikely to happen again in the future? Let's look at some secondary details:

1. The firm had left several questions blank on the application they submitted. This alone wouldn't cause us to decline coverage if we otherwise like the risk. Companies typically only see these applications once per year, and there are insurance terms that they may not be familiar with. They may need help from their insurance agent to complete some of the questions.

2. The firm had a prior E&O policy that was canceled for non-payment of premium. But then again, this wouldn't necessarily cause us to decline coverage, depending on the circumstances. The issue may lie with the law firm's insurance agent, or there may have been some fluke administrative issue. They are now current with their payments, so there is no active issue there.

3. The application looks like the law partner who filled it out wrote with his non-dominant hand during a bumpy car ride. Again, this one on its own wouldn't cause us to decline a risk we otherwise like, although it's not ideal.

4. When providing information about the $250,000 claim, the attorney used some less-than-ideal verbiage – describing the client as a "jerk" and "impossible to get a hold of."

The bottom line is, we chose not to offer this firm coverage. Yes, they had missed a deadline and been sued for a quarter of a million dollars, but there are lots of firms who fit that profile that we do offer to cover.

What we have here is corroboration. Corroboration is "evidence which confirms or supports a statement, theory, or finding". This firm appeared sloppy based on its costly mistake. While none of the items identified individually make or break our decision about whether to offer coverage, they all corroborate that finding.

Let's apply this to the matter at hand. The direct evidence we've reviewed to this point shows that the Bible is the authoritative Word of God. There is also secondary (or indirect) evidence that corroborates this finding. Specifically, I'm referring to archaeology and non-Christian ancient writings.

Archaeology

Pastor Voddie Bauchum sums up the argument in one statement. "There have been 25,000 archaeological digs related directly to the subject matter in the Bible. Not one has contradicted the Bible. The overwhelming majority have confirmed and affirmed something in the Bible."[1] Whereas archaeology has been catastrophic for other religions, it continues to corroborate the evidence for the Bible.[2] I use the term "continues" because there are beliefs and opinions of skeptics that continue to be demolished based on evidence that archeologists unearth.

One impressive example relates to Luke, the aforementioned author of the Gospel of Luke and the Book of Acts in the Bible. Luke was the historian who wrote his gospel by carefully tracing information provided by multiple eyewitnesses. In *The Case for Christ*, Lee Strobel explains how a prominent archaeologist was able to verify Luke's references

---

1. Youtube- Voddie Bauchum- Why I Choose to Believe the Bible

2. Apologists like Lee Strobel, J. Warner Wallace, and Frank Turek argue that archaeology proves Mormonism is demonstrably FALSE.

to 32 countries, 54 cities, and 9 islands. In all of these examples, he made ZERO mistakes. Further, Roman historian, Colin Hemer, used archaeology to verify obscure details Luke included that could only come from eyewitnesses – things like "small-town politicians, local slang, topographical features, specific weather patterns, and even water depths." [3] With inconsequential and obscure details proven 100% correct, am I to believe that Luke was careless in tracing the eyewitness accounts of the resurrection of Jesus? I don't think so.

Non-Christian Ancient Writings

Ten non-Christian writers mention Jesus within 150 years of his life. These non-Christian authors could be characterized as ranging from neutral to decidedly anti-Christian. They include Josephus, perhaps the most significant Jewish historian of his time. From these non-Christian authors alone, we would know things about Jesus such as: [4]

- He lived a moral life.

- He performed miracles.

- He was crucified.

- Darkness and an earthquake occurred when he died.

- He was acclaimed to be the Messiah.

- His followers believed he rose from the dead.

- His followers were willing to die specifically for that belief.

---

3. Stealing from God, Frank Turek

4. I Don't Have Enough Faith to be an Atheist, Frank Turek

- His followers denied the Roman (false) gods and wor-shipped Jesus as God.

- Christianity spread rapidly.

That information is all attested by non-Christians, including anti-Christian sources. For example, the writings don't say that Jesus rose from the dead. Otherwise, it would be Christian writing. Instead, they say that Jesus' followers believed He rose from the dead, and they were willing to die for that belief. That makes absolutely no sense unless it's true, but that's a story for another book (namely, Jesus: Fib, Dead, or God? in this series!).

The bottom line is that, the writings of 10 ancient non-Christian authors support what the Bible says. In our modern age, the figure of 10 authors may not sound all that impressive. For context, we must understand that Tiberius Caesar, the Roman Emperor at the time, was also only referenced by ten ancient authors! Let's use the classic essay, "One Solitary Life" to put this into perspective:

"Here is a man who was born in an obscure village, the child of a peasant woman. He grew up in another village. He worked in a carpenter ship until He was thirty. Then for three years, He was an itinerant preacher. He never owned a home. He never wrote a book. He never held an office. He never had a family. He never went to college. He never put His foot inside a big city. He never traveled two hundred miles from the place He was born. He never did one of the things that usually accompany greatness. He had no credentials but Himself...." **He was written about as much as the Emperor of Rome**. Really? By the way, when you add in Christian writers, Jesus was referenced by 42 sources in total, or four times more than Tiberius Caesar. That's like a 19th-century carpenter from Des Moines being written about more than Abraham Lincoln.

Friend, the evidence for the Bible is indeed corroborated. Again, let's add it to our notes and move on.

Risk Characteristics:
1. **C**ollection

2. **O**ut in front of science

3. **R**esilient

4. **R**evered

5. **E**yewitness

6. **C**orroborated

Chapter Ten

THOUSANDS

The focus of this section has been on risk characteristics that are used by underwriters to pick "winners." The other critical responsibility of underwriters is choosing how much to charge for each policy. To do so, I typically set up a dartboard on my wall, play a round or two, and just issue quotes based on wherever the darts stick.

I'm kidding.

Pricing for risk is actually very complex. First, information about the applicant company is run through a proprietary rating program to determine a "base rate." From there, underwriters have the discretion to apply debits (which increase the price) and credits (which decrease the price).

Debits are generally applied to reflect a company's claims history. Several factors are considered; including the number of claims, the payouts, the age of the claims, and any unique circumstances. On the other side of the ledger, credits are applied to reward favorable risk characteristics. This includes things like many years' experience, utilizing best practices, keeping risk management protocols in place, and so forth.

As an underwriter, I'm on the front lines. I use our rating programs to price out policies for companies that apply for coverage. That said, a tremendous amount of "behind the scenes" work goes into creating, maintaining, and monitoring these rating programs. That work is done mainly by *actuaries*.

Actuaries are professionals involved in virtually every aspect of an insurance company's operations. They are typically experts in statistics and finance. If you think about the top 10 students in your math class growing up, one or more of them is probably an actuary today. Actuaries crunch all the numbers to determine what the insurance company needs to do to be profitable. That involves pricing the policies, determining how much the insurance company should invest, and setting "reserves." Reserves are the funds that insurance companies set aside to ensure they have enough money to pay claims for policyholders who get sued.

If there is one thing that actuaries love, it's data. The more of it, the better. Actuaries analyze staggering amounts of data to help the company make informed, fact-based decisions. This includes up-front guidance on how much to charge and ongoing updates on how we're doing. They study past data and search for trends to predict future financial loss. Finally, they closely monitor our results to make sure what we're doing is working.

Earlier, I stated that there is an "art and a science" to underwriting - this is the science. And its importance can't be overstated. Data equals knowledge. And when it comes to data, we're generally asking two questions:

1. Do we have a lot of it?

2. Is the quality acceptable?

It's not unusual for an actuary to report results along with a word of caution that we shouldn't draw any sweeping conclusions from the findings because the data is still "too green." In other words, the data is too new to be trusted, and there's not enough of it to rely upon.

The bottom line is that, more quality data means less uncertainty. And when it comes to ancient documents, quality data means having lots of manuscripts written not long after the original document. So the more manuscripts we have and the earlier those manuscripts are (relative to when the original was written), the more trustworthy the data will be.

So how does the Bible stack up?

In a word, dominant. No other ancient document is even in the ballpark. The Bible has more manuscripts and earlier manuscripts than the next best ten pieces of classical literature combined. Here's the breakdown:

> Homer, Demosthenes, Herodotus, Plato, Tacitus, Caesar, and Pliny have about 2,100 manuscripts combined. The Bible has about 5,700. Those same authors have an average time gap of 1,000 years between the original document and the first surviving copies. The Bible's is 25 years. [1]

A review of the data shows there is no real comparison. As I read the reports, the first thing that came to mind was the "mercy rule" from my son's Little League baseball games. The "mercy rule" is put in place for youth sports, so the scores don't get out of hand in lopsided competitions. It ends the

---

1. Frank Turek, "I Don't Have Enough Faith to be an Atheist"

game earlier than scheduled when one team has a huge, insurmountable lead. If this thing were a game, we would've hit the "mercy rule" long ago.

We know that a high volume of high-quality data helps reduce uncertainty and make fact-based decisions. Therefore, the thousands of early manuscripts make a compelling case for the Bible. In the next section, we will dig deeper into the specifics of why it matters. But, for now, let's note this final risk characteristic and assess our progress thus far.

Risk Characteristics:

- **C**ollection

- **O**ut in front of science

- **R**esilient

- **R**evered

- **E**yewitness

- **C**orroborated

- **T**housands

Where we stand

In Part 1 (Triage), we took the critical first step of triaging the 10,000+ religions on the planet. They can't all be true because they make conflicting claims. Therefore, we gave ourselves the best chance of finding truth by directing our efforts by the guidance of the Son of God. Our eligibility requirement is that the book(s) must be endorsed by Jesus Christ. Only the Bible passes this test, as Jesus taught it is more important than physical sustenance.

With the triage complete and only one holy text left standing, we were able to focus our efforts and crank up the heat on our review of the Bible. In Part 2 (Underwriting), we underwrote the text by taking a closer look at some specific risk characteristics. We found that the Bible is a **C**ollection, **O**ut in front of science, **R**esilient, **R**evered, **E**yewitness, **C**orroborated, and that there are **T**housands of manuscripts. In other words, the Bible is **CORRECT.**

It's time to we move on to Referrals. With complex assignments, there are often questions, concerns, and potential red flags that fall outside the individual underwriter's authority. These issues are referred to a superior who can review and, if acceptable, approve them. That's where we're headed. Let's roll.

REFERRALS

REFERRALS

"In this business, there's not a lot of things that will get you fired. But lying is one."

I was fresh out of college, hired into my first "real job" as an underwriter trainee. My manager was recounting a story of an underwriter who had broached his underwriting authority. In other words, the underwriter got caught quoting insurance policies without the proper authorization. His manager gave him a chance to come clean, but instead, he doubled down on his lie. In the end, he was terminated.

Authority is one of the first things that new underwriters learn about. Every underwriter receives a Letter of Authority that clearly establishes which decisions fall within their purview, and which need to be elevated to a superior for written approval. This authority level is delegated by the Chief Underwriting Officer and reflects the underwriter's technical level. For instance, brand new underwriters typically need signoff for 100% of the quotes that they issue. The underwriter can earn increased authority with time, more experience, and demonstrated competence. Ultimately, the entire process revolves around trust. Trust is valuable because it's hard to earn and easy to lose. It also takes time to acquire and can be lost in a heartbeat.

The Letters of Authority allow underwriters varying levels of autonomy to make decisions while also serving as a system of checks and balances. When a particular risk factor falls outside of the underwriter's authority, it is their responsibility to "refer" that item to their superior for written approval. For instance, a new underwriter may earn authority to issue quotes to companies with no claims filed in the past five years. But suppose the underwriter wants to issue a quote to a company with a recent claim. Then, they must send a "referral" to their superior to get written signoff to proceed.

In most organizations, the highest level in the chain of command for underwriting decisions is the Chief Underwriting Officer (CUO). The CUO is responsible for managing the company's underwriting performance.

Interestingly, when it comes to the word of God, we too have a Chief who has full authority...

> "Then the eleven disciples went to Galilee, to the mountain where Jesus told them to go. When they saw Him, they worshipped Him; but some doubted. Then Jesus came to them and said, '**All authority in heaven and on earth has been given to me**. Therefore, go and make disciples of all nations, baptizing them in the name of the Father and of the Son and of the Holy Spirit, and teaching them to obey everything I have commanded you. And surely, I am with you always, to the very end of the age.'"[1]

---

1. Matthew 28:16

The buck stops with the Chief. So, as we run into potential red flags associated with the Bible, it's only right that we "refer" the issues to Him for approval. And there is no shortage of red flags. Perhaps you've heard that the Bible is full of contradictions and errors. Or that it's been translated so many times that we have no idea what the original said anyway. But it's just as well because the Bible promotes things like prejudice, genocide, and slavery. It's anti-science, anti-intellectual, and anti-women. It sure sounds like a dangerous book!

We've got a lot to tackle here, friend. First, if we're to proceed, our risk evaluation needs:

1. **Red Flags**- the underwriter must identify questions, concerns, and potential red flags they came across in their underwriting.

2. **Rationale**- the underwriter must explain what information has resolved the question/concern/potential red flag.

3. **Written Approval**- if the CUO signs off on it, the underwriter must document the file with their written approval.

That's exactly what we'll do together here in Part 3. Let's get to work.

Chapter Eleven

"BUT THE BIBLE IS FULL OF ERRORS..."

"*Men Walk on Moon*" was the front-page headline of the New York Times on Monday, July 21, 1969. I referenced the original article and typed out the excerpt below for our review. However, after typing out the passage, I realized I had made an error. Therefore, my version is slightly different than what was actually printed in the newspaper. Can you identify the mistake? No googling allowed!

MEN WALK ON MOON

Houston, Monday, July 21—Men have landed and walked on the moon. Two Americans, astronauts of Apollo 11, steered their fragile four-legged lunar module safely and smoothly to a historic landing, yesterday at 4:17:40 P.M. , Eastern daylight time. Neil A. Armstrong, the 38-year-old civilian commander, radioed to earth and the mission control room here: "Houston, Tranquility Base here. The Eagle has landed." The first men to reach the moon—Mr. Armstrong and his co-pilot, Col. Edwin E. Aldrin, Jr. of the Air Force—brought their ship to rest on a level, rock-strewn plain near the southwestern shore of the arid Sea of Tranquility. About six and a half hours later, Mr. Armstrong opened the landing craft's hatch, stepped slowly down the ladder and declared as he planted the first human footprint on the lunar crust: "That's one small step for man, one giant leap for mankind." His first step on the moon came at 10:56:20 P.M., as a television camera outside the craft transmitted his every move to an awed and excited audience of hundreds of millions of people on earth.

Did you find it? In the second line, I typed that the astronauts "steered their fragile four-legged lunar module safely and smoothly to *a* historic landing..." It's supposed to say that the astronauts steered their fragile four-legged lunar module safely and smoothly to *the* historic landing.

This was front-page news describing one of the most important events of the 20th century. The original source is The New York Times, which has won "132 Pulitzer Prizes, the most of any newspaper, and has long been regarded within the industry as a national 'newspaper of record'." So, with all of that in mind, I have to ask. How could you have missed my blatant mistake?

If this exercise seems a bit ridiculous to you, I agree. You may be thinking, "How could I have possibly caught that error without having the original, correct version in front of me to check it against?"

And that, my friend, is precisely the point.

To claim that there are errors in a document implies that you know what the correct version says.

So how can you say there are errors if you don't know what the correct version says?

It's here that our red flag stalls out before it even gets started. One of the most common objections to the Bible is that it's filled with "errors." How could someone know that unless they knew what the original said?

They can't.

So, we can toss this objection out the window to begin with, but let's continue further.[1] This objection is rooted in the idea that, even if the originals were the word of God, we no longer have the originals. It is true that we don't have any of the actual papers that a Biblical writer wrote on. What we have are handwritten copies of the documents called manuscripts. Because of the materials they were written on, this is the case for **all** significant literature from the ancient world. Recall, however, that we have more manuscripts and earlier manuscripts of the Bible than the next best ten pieces of classical literature combined. And this is one of the reasons it's important. This rich data allows scholars to reconstruct the original documents easily. Let's take our previous example and see if you can crack the code using these hypothetical copies:

Manuscript 1: Two Americans, astronauts of Apollo 11, steered their fragile four-legged lunar module safely and smoothly to t#e historic landing yesterday at 4:17:40 P.M., Eastern daylight time

Manuscript 2: Two Americans, astronauts of Apollo 11, steered their fragile four-legged lunar module safely and smoothly to #he historic landing yesterday at 4:17:40 P.M., Eastern daylight time

---

1. This section detailed in Chapter 9 of "I Don't Have Enough Faith to be an Atheist"

Manuscript 3: Two Americans, astronauts of Apollo 11, steered their fragile four-legged lunar module safely and smoothly to th# historic landing yesterday at 4:17:40 P.M., Eastern daylight time

Manuscript 4: Two Americans, astronauts of Apollo 11, steered their fragile four-legged lunar module safely and smoothly to a historic landing yesterday at 4:17:40 P.M., Eastern daylight time

Manuscript 5: Two Americans, astronauts of Apollo 11, steered their fragile four-legged lunar module safely and smoothly t# the historic landing yesterday at 4:17:40 P.M., Eastern daylight time

Do you see how having multiple early copies can be used to reconstruct the original? This type of work, called textual criticism, is done by specialist scholars. These scholars have essentially put the matter of whether we have an accurate copy of the original documents to bed. The Bible wasn't printed until 1455, so everything we have before that is handwritten by scribes. At one time, some critics alleged that there were 150,000 copying "errors" in the New Testament documents alone. Textual scholars straightened that out. For instance, the vast majority of the so-called "errors" are strictly grammatical, like punctuation and spelling. Also, the 150,000 "errors" are spread out amongst 5,700 manuscripts, so "one letter of one word in one verse in 2,000 manuscripts is counted as 2,000 errors."

One final nail in the coffin of this objection is the writings of the early church fathers. Leaders like Clement, Ignatius, and Polycarp constantly quoted New Testament books in their letters.

Amazingly, we can reproduce all but 11 verses of the entire New Testament using <u>only</u> the writings of the early church fathers.[2]

The bottom line is that, the New Testament documents have been authenticated.

To close this referral, we'll return to our example. You may be thinking that this is a whole lot of work for an "error" that makes absolutely no difference to your reading of the sentence. Whether they "steered their fragile four-legged lunar modular safely and smoothly to 'a' historic landing, or to 'the' historic landing", makes no difference to the point that's being conveyed.

Again, I agree with you. And the same holds true for the so-called errors in the New Testament documents. Textual scholars have confirmed that not a single one of the 150,000 alleged "errors" affects "an article of faith or a precept of duty which is not abundantly sustained by other and undoubted passaged, or by the whole tenor of Scripture teaching."

Bottom line: we know with 99.5% accuracy exactly what the original New Testament documents said, and the .5% doesn't impact any doctrine of the Christian faith.[3]

Referral: The Bible isn't reliable because it's full of errors.

CUO Approval: "For truly I tell you, until heaven and earth disappear, not the smallest letter, not the least stroke of a

---

2. Clement, Ignatius, Polycarp- as detailed in Voddie "Why I believe the Bible" and "I don't have enough faith to be an atheist"

3. William Lane Craig

pen, will by any means disappear from the Law until everything is accomplished." [4]

***

---

4. Matthew 5:18 NIV

Chapter Twelve

"BUT IT'S BEEN TRANSLATED SO MANY TIMES..."

Nike's global sales were over $40 billion last year. Surely, co-founder Bill Bowerman could never have imagined such a figure as he sat at his kitchen table for breakfast nearly 50 years ago. Bill was the running coach at the University of Oregon and was looking for new shoes. The team's track was transitioning to a new surface, and Bill needed a shoe that would be suitable to handle it. Bill's wife recounted the story years later, "As one of the waffles came out, he said, 'You know, by turning it upside down—where the waffle part would come in contact with the track—I think that might work.' So he got up from the table and went tearing into his lab. He reached for two cans of whatever it is you pour together to make the urethane, and poured them into the waffle iron."[1]

---

1. https://www.highsnobiety.com/p/nike-waffle-trainer-history/

The rest is history. The Nike "waffle" rubber sole was born and successfully released in 1973. The early versions were crude, but they were a hit in the track & field community nonetheless. The sole was updated and used in various Nike products over the years. Nike even recently released a *Waffle Trainer 2* as an homage to the iconic rubber soles.

Of course, running technology has come a long way since Bill Bowerman cooked up this innovation a half-century ago. Any runner can tell you that if there is one thing shoemakers do, it's iteration. They are constantly innovating and updating their shoes. For instance, Nike's most popular running shoe, the Air Pegasus, was launched in 1983. In 1985, a lighter version, Pegasus GX, was released. In 1987, the Pegasus 3 launched with increased cushioning. In 1989, the Air Pegasus was launched in a wider range of colors. Fast forward to today, and you can purchase the Nike Air Zoom Pegasus **38's** in your local shoe store.[2]

The thirty-eighth installment of the same shoe! And with every model, changes are made as the technology gets more advanced. So I'm sure Nike has the thirty-eight's in their laboratories now, working to improve them for the next model. And after they release the 39's, they'll have those in the lab, working on the 40's.

When it comes to running shoes, this is a wonderful process. When it comes to the Bible, not so much. In fact, it's a significant problem. Many people mistakenly believe that this is the type of process the Bible goes through when it is translated. So for example, when I first heard of the New King James Version of the Bible, I just assumed that they had taken the King James Version and modified it. But that's not how it works.

2. https://sustainhealth.fit/

It's not like shoes, where the Nike engineers modify the previous year's model. Biblical scholars aren't modifying the most recent translation. Instead, every time a new translation is done, the scholars go back and base their work off of those original 5,700 early manuscripts we previously discussed. The same original Greek, Hebrew, and Aramaic manuscripts are the starting point for every translation.

Unfortunately, critics perpetuate this mistake by portraying the translation process as if it were a "telephone game." You may be familiar with this classic game, often used as an ice-breaker for groups. Basically, someone chooses a word or phrase and whispers it to the person next to them. That person, in turn, whispers it to the next person, and so forth. The fun is to see how much the message changes by the time it reaches the last person in the group. Unfortunately, this type of slander leads to the common assertion that the Bible isn't reliable because "it's been translated so many times." Pastor Voddie Bauchum concluded that, anyone making this assertion is either "ignorant, evil, or both", since it doesn't reflect how translations are actually done.

When put in proper context, an objection to Bible translations in and of itself doesn't even make sense. Jesus left His followers with the direct command to, "Go and make disciples of **all nations**, baptizing them in the name of the Father, and of the Son, and of the Holy Spirit." [3] Am I to believe that command meant teaching everyone on earth how to read Greek, Hebrew, and Aramaic? Of course not. It's inherent in the command from Jesus that the Bible must be translated.

---

3. The Great Commission, Matthew 28:18

In summary, Bible translation is nothing like a game of telephone. Rather, it's a powerful tactic used to complete the assignment Jesus left for us.

Let's return to Pastor Voddie to put a bow on this issue. "This bothers me a great deal. It bothers me that there are people who claim to be intelligent, yet continue to make this argument. And it bothers me that there are Christians who don't laugh at them."

Referral: The Bible isn't reliable because it's been translated so many times.

CUO Approval: "Then Jesus came to them and said, 'All authority in heaven and on earth has been given to me. Therefore, go and make disciples of all nations, baptizing them in the name of the Father and of the Son and of the Holy Spirit'." [4]

---

4. Matthew 28:18

Chapter Thirteen

"BUT IT WAS WRITTEN BY MEN... PART 1"

With over 4 million copies sold, *The First Days of School: How to Be an Effective Teacher* is the all-time best-selling book on classroom management. It is the "most requested book for what works in the classroom for teachers' and students' success." It's been translated into 8 languages and used in over 120 countries. The book has over 1,400 reviews on Amazon and boasts an average of 4.6 out of 5 stars. Profits from the book fund a non-profit school built in the jungles of Cambodia. And the author, Harry K. Wong, was named one of the "Twenty Most Admired People in Education" by Instructor Magazine.

Unfortunately, this book was written by a human, so it's not reliable.

"The Total Money Makeover: A Proven Plan for Financial Fitness" is a New York Times Best Seller. It has helped millions of people develop "everyday money-saving habits and become financially healthy for life." The author, Dave Ramsey, has a personal finance radio show that is listened to by over 23 million people every week. In addition, he has written seven national best-selling books, and his Financial Peace program

has helped over 6 million families get out of debt and change their lives.

Unfortunately, this book was written by a human, so it's not reliable.

"How to Win Friends and Influence People" is a self-help book first published in 1936. It was an instant hit, selling over 250,000 copies within three months of being released. With over 30 million copies sold worldwide, it is one of the best-selling books of all time. It was released almost 90 years ago, and it still sells about 250,000 copies a year. It is considered one of the most influential books in American history.

Unfortunately, this book was written by a human, so it's not reliable.

Cornelius Tacitus is regarded as one of the greatest Roman historians by modern scholars. His book, *"Annals"*, is considered his most outstanding work and is an important source for the modern understanding of the Roman Empire during the first century.

Unfortunately, this book was written by a human, so it's not reliable.

"Night" is a 1960 memoir written by Holocaust survivor Elie Wiesel. Wiesel details his experiences at the Nazi Concentration Camps of Auschwitz and Buchenwald. The book has been translated into 30 languages and is considered one of the "bedrocks of Holocaust literature".

Unfortunately, this book was written by a human, so it's not reliable.

"The Making of the Atomic Bomb" won a Pulitzer Prize for General Non-Fiction, the National Book Award for Non-Fic-

tion, and a National Critic's Circle Award. The book is praised both by historians, weapons engineers, and scientists. It is considered the "authority on early weapons history, as well as the development of modern physics in general."

Unfortunately, this book was written by a human, so it's not reliable.

"The Souls of Black Folk: Essays and Drawings" is "a seminal work in the history of sociology and a cornerstone of African-American literature." W.E.B. Du Bois drew on his personal experience as an African-American in American society to write about race.

Unfortunately, this book was written by a human, so it's not reliable.

Does this analysis strike you as flawed? I would say so, yet this reasoning is used as a widespread objection against the Bible. Skeptics claim that they can't trust the Bible because "it was written by man." Meanwhile, the knowledge that the skeptic possesses on *every other subject* comes from text written by man. To summarily dismiss a text because it was written by man means that ALL text must be rejected. By this logic, everything you've ever read is unreliable. This objection is way too broad. Who or what *would* the text need to be written by, to convince the skeptic? A magic wand?

The Bible says that "all scripture is God breathed." [1] In other words, God wrote it. But what do we mean by that? It does not mean we believe that God physically put pen to paper and wrote it down. Of course, He could have, seeing as He created the pen, the paper, and everything else in the universe from nothing. But that's not what we believe. Nor does

---

1. 2 Timothy 3:16

it mean that God dictated the words, and the 40+ human authors simply acted like robotic courtroom stenographers. We're informed by 2 Peter 3: 19-21:

"We also have the prophetic message as something completely reliable, and you will do well to pay attention to it, as to a light shining in a dark place, until the day dawns and the morning rises in your hearts. Above all, you must understand that no prophecy of Scripture came about by the prophet's own interpretation of things. For prophecy never had its origin in the human will, but prophets, though human, spoke from God as they were carried along by the Holy Spirit."

Ding, ding, ding! Now we're talking. When we say God wrote the Bible, we mean:

God inspired men to write down exactly what He wanted them to, without violating their personalities. [2]

It's here where our understanding of God's inspiration of the Bible lies. And we've seen that to claim the Bible is unreliable because "it was written by man," is nonsensical. So we're ready to bring this one to the Chief for signoff.

Referral: The Bible isn't reliable because it was written by men- Part 1

---

2. YouTube: Wretched: Atheist Objection: The Bible is unreliable because it was written by men

CUO Approval: Jesus responded, "Then why does **David, speaking under the inspiration of the Spirit,** call the Messiah 'my Lord?'" [3]

***

---

3. Matthew 22:43 NLT

Chapter Fourteen

"BUT IT WAS WRITTEN BY MEN... PART 2"

M eteorologists use advanced technology to help predict the weather forecast. As their technology improves, so does the accuracy of their predictions. Today, forecasters use: [1]

- **Doppler Radar**- there are now hundreds of radar towers installed across the United States. These towers emit bursts of energy, which will bounce off of and detect precipitation in the air. Computers then "listen" for the response and analyze the data.

- **Satellite Data**- three different types of satellites monitor weather activity from space and send data for scientists to analyze. Polar-orbiting satellites take 6-7 detailed images per day, geostationary satellites stay high above the Earth and take images as soon as every 30 seconds, and deep space satellites face the sun to monitor storms in space.

- **Radiosondes**- twice a day, radiosondes are tied to

1. https://www.noaa.gov

weather balloons in nearly 100 locations across the US. They are launched and travel for 2 hours, providing air data back to scientists.

- **Automated Surface Observing Systems**- these tools constantly monitor the weather on the Earth's surface. More than 900 of these stations report weather data up to 12 times per hour.

- **Supercomputers**- according to the National Oceanic and Atmospheric Association, these are the "backbone of modern forecasting." These computers are about 6 million times more powerful than the computer I'm typing from, now.

- **Advanced Weather Information Processing System**- this tool combines the data from all of the previously mentioned tools and presents them in a dashboard format.

Talk about advanced science. With all of this weather predicting technology available, we're now able to...

Achieve a 50/50 chance of accurately predicting a 10-day weather forecast.[2]

In other words, it is pretty much the same chance if you were to simply flip a coin. As a youth baseball coach here in New England, I can safely say that this comes as no surprise to me at all. Baseball coaches are constantly monitoring the weather to determine whether their practices and games will be on as scheduled or canceled. We have the responsibility of notifying parents in a timely manner to the best of our ability. With this responsibility, I began to see just how volatile the

2. https://scijinks.gov/forecast-reliability/

weather forecasts could be. I rarely look ahead more than a couple of days because the forecast seems to be of little use at that point.

Is that due to a lack of technology? Clearly not. Is it because the meteorologists are lazy and bad at their jobs? Of course not. These are professionals who are dedicated to their craft. Here's what it comes down to:

We can't predict the future!

Of course, there are all sorts of areas that we use data and trends to *try* to broadly forecast what's coming. Still, humans cannot predict the future with great specificity. Who can predict the future but God?

"Remember the former things, those of long ago; I am God, and there is no other; I am God, and there is none like me. I make known the end from the beginning, from ancient times, what is still to come, I say, 'My purpose will stand, and I will do all that I please.' From the east I summon a bird of prey; from a far-off land, a man to fulfill my purpose. What I have said, that I will bring about; what I have planned, that I will do." [3]

Fulfilled prophecies are yet another marker that the Bible is not simply "written by men." According to Pastor John MacArthur, "You can't find in any other religious book in the world that has well-attested and accurate fulfilled prophecy." Meanwhile, Bible scholars cite 1,000 prophecies in scripture, many of them already fulfilled. These prophecies run the gamut in terms of topic, but perhaps, no category is more compelling than Messianic Prophecy.

---

3. Isaiah 46: 9-11

God promised the nation of Israel that He would deliver a Savior who would sit on the throne forever. This Savior is known as the Messiah, or "anointed one." For hundreds of years, God delivered messages about this Messiah, using prophets. There are at least 60 *specific* Messianic Prophecies in the Old Testament. I emphasize "specific" because these are not vague, generalized predictions. Isaiah 53, for example, was written 700 years before the birth of Jesus, yet till today, it reads like it could be his biography. To give you a better idea of the level of specificity we're talking about, there are Messianic Prophecies in the Bible that indicate that the Messiah will:

- **Be born of a virgin**- *Therefore the Lord himself will give you a sign: The virgin will conceive and give birth to a son, and will call him Immanuel (God with us).* [4]

- **Be born in the tiny town of Bethlehem**- *But you, Bethlehem, Though you are little among the thousands of Judah, Yet out of you shall come forth to Me, The One to be Ruler in Israel, Whose going forth are from of old, From Everlasting.* [5]

- **Be a miracle worker**- *Then will the eyes of the blind be opened and the ears of the deaf unstopped, then the lame will leap like a deer and the mute tongue shout for joy.* [6]

---

4. Isaiah 7:14

5. Micah 5:1

6. Isaiah 35:5

- **Be executed among sinners**- *He poured out his life unto death and was numbered with the transgressors.*[7]

- **Pray for His persecutors**- *He bore the sin of many and made intercession for the transgressors.*[7]

- **Have His hands and feet pierced**- *Dogs surround me, a pack of villains encircles me, they pierce my hands and my feet.*[9]

- **Be raised from the dead, go up to heaven, and be seated at the right hand of the Father-** *The Lord says to my Lord, sit at my right hand until I make your enemies a footstool for your feet.*[10]

Does that sound like anyone you know? These are specific prophecies that appear in the Old Testament. They were written *hundreds of years* before Jesus was born, and we then see them fulfilled in the New Testament.

People don't write books that predict the future with specificity. So, we have what we need to refer this one up to the Chief.

Referral: The Bible isn't reliable because it's written by men- Part 2.

---

7. Isaiah 53:12

7. Isaiah 53:12

9. Psalm 22:16

10. Psalm 110:1

CUO Approval: "Do not think that I have come to abolish the Law or the Prophets; I have not come to abolish them but to fulfill them." [11]

***

---

11. Matthew 5:17

Chapter Fifteen

"BUT OVERZEALOUS MONKS EDITED IT..."

*T*he War of the Worlds is a science-fiction novel by HG Wells. The story was originally released in 1897 and centers around Martians invading England. The Martians overwhelm the British army with sophisticated weapons, a "heat-ray," and poisonous smoke. Ultimately, the Martians are betrayed by their lack of an immune system and are wiped out by Earthly diseases. The novel is said to be a satire of British imperialism, and it spawned an entire genre of science fiction in England.[1]

We probably would never have heard of it if the story ended there. But if we fast forward about 40 years, things get interesting. Twenty-three-year-old Orson Welles selected the novel for his "Mercury Theatre on Air" radio program, which was known for re-imagining literary classics. His adaptation of the novel involved a series of fake news bulletins that described a Martian invasion of New Jersey, Chicago, and St. Louis.

---

1. https://www.smithsonianmag.com/

Soon, an announcer was at the (New Jersey) crash site describing a Martian emerging from a large metallic cylinder. "Good heavens," he declared, "something's wriggling out of the shadow like a gray snake. Now here's another and another one and another one. They look like tentacles to me ... I can see the thing's body now. It's large, large as a bear. It glistens like wet leather. But that face, it... it ... ladies and gentlemen, it's indescribable. I can hardly force myself to keep looking at it, it's so awful. The eyes are black and gleam like a serpent. The mouth is kind of V-shaped with saliva dripping from its rimless lips that seem to quiver and pulsate."[2]

Yikes. Unfortunately, not everyone listening realized that this was a work of fiction. With much of the country on edge in the time leading up to World War II, the performance struck a nerve. Thousands of people breathlessly shared the reports with others, and some even fled from their homes. Police stations were overwhelmed with phone calls asking if the invasion was real, and by the following day, the hoax was front-page news from coast to coast.

All because of a work of fiction. A fantasy.

Interestingly, we've seen works of fiction that have also deceived people with respect to the Bible. Various "realistic" works of fantasy have perpetuated a series of objections related to which texts are included in the Bible and whether or not they are accurate.

For example, skeptics latch onto conspiracy theories involving "other" gospels that are not included in the Bible. These "other" gospels typically have some "secret information" that goes against an orthodox Christian belief – such as Jesus being human and not divine. Another book in this

2. https://www.history.com

series is dedicated to explaining why Christians believe that Jesus is exactly who He said He is, the Son of God. But for our purposes here, we can point out that the "other" gospels were second-century writings not written by eyewitnesses. The writers give themselves away by making all sorts of mistakes even about the local geography because; (1) they weren't actually there, and (2) they were writing centuries later. The "other" gospels bear the names of Apostles, just as counterfeit products bear the logos of established brands. It was a strategy of the plagiarists to use the names of Apostles in an effort to pass their text off as authoritative. For instance, the "Gospel of Thomas" would be a fantastic feat for the Apostle Thomas to have written, seeing as it was done about 100 years after he had died.

Another derivative of this type of objection would go something along the lines of, "The books of the New Testament weren't chosen until the 4th-century church councils." We know that's not the case, thanks to the previously referenced writings of the early church fathers. By 108 AD, the early church fathers had already written commentaries on and quoted 25 of the 27 books of the New Testament! That's a cool 200+ years, before the Bible councils in the fourth century. The reason the councils didn't happen until the fourth century is because of the intense persecution facing Christians until that time. It wasn't until the Edict of Milan in 313 AD, that Christianity was deemed "tolerable" within the Roman Empire.

As world-class Bible scholar Bruce Metzger puts it, "The canon is a list of authoritative books more than it is an authoritative list of books." It's not as if the idea of Jesus' resurrection was something new that sprang up out of these councils in the fourth century.

A third and final example of an objection to the Bible arising out of works of fantasy is the "Overzealous Monks

Theory." This one basically says that the Bible only *appears* totally consistent because there were overzealous monks during the time of Constantine who edited out anything unfavorable. This is implausible on several levels:[3]

1. As you know by now, there were more early manuscripts of the New Testament documents than the next ten best combined. That means that these fourth-century monks would need to track down all ~5,700 early manuscripts, change them all, not get caught, return them, and keep the conspiracy a secret forever.

2. By the fourth century, the New Testament had been translated into Syriac, Coptic, and Latin. After tracking down the ~5,700 early manuscripts and doctoring those, the monks would need to learn how to tell the same lies in three additional languages. They would need to track down the translated versions and change those to match the lies they told on the original Greek manuscripts. Again, this is assuming they don't get caught, return them, and keep the conspiracy a secret forever.

3. Don't forget about the prolific writings of the early church fathers. We can reconstruct all but 11 verses of the New Testament using their commentaries and quotations alone. Thus, the overzealous monks would need to track these down to doctor them up also. They'd need those commentaries to make sure they match all the lies that were told previously in Greek, Syriac, Coptic, and Latin. And again, this assumes they don't get caught, can return the docu-

---

3. Derived from Pastor Voddie Bauchum's research and sermons

ments undetected, and keep the conspiracy a secret forever.

I don't believe there is a whole lot more that needs to be added here. Let's refer it to the Chief for approval.

Referral: Fine, the Bible seems consistent. But only because overzealous monks edited the New Testament during the time of Constantine...

CUO Approval: "Heaven and earth will pass away, but my words will never pass away."[4]

---

4. Matthew 22:35 NIV

Chapter Sixteen

"BUT THE BIBLE IS FULL OF CONTRADICTIONS.."

O f the 2,223 passengers on board the Titanic, only 706 survived. Many of the survivors watched the ship go down from their lifeboats. Here are some eyewitness accounts of what they saw and heard:[1]

Charles Herbert Lightoller, 2nd Officer on Collapsible B

Senator Smith. Was the vessel broken in two in any manner, or intact?
  Mr. Lightoller. Absolutely intact.
  Senator Smith. On the decks?
  Mr. Lightoller. Intact, sir.

Herbert John Pitman, 3rd Officer in Lifeboat 5

1. https://www.encyclopedia-titanica.org

Mr. Pitman. Judging by what I could see from a distance, she gradually disappeared until the forecastle head was submerged to the bridge. Then she turned right on end and went down perpendicularly.

Senator Smith. Did she seem to be broken in two?

Mr. Pitman. Oh, no.

Frank Osman, Seaman in Lifeboat 2

Mr. Osman. We pulled astern that way again, and after we got astern, we lay on our oars and saw the ship go down. After she got to a certain angle she exploded; broke in halves, and it seemed to me as if all the engines and everything that was in the after part slid out into the forward part, and the after part came up right again, and as soon as it came up right, down it went again.

George Moore, Seaman in Lifeboat 3

Senator Newlands. How far were you from the ship when it sank?

Mr. Moore. I should say just over a quarter of a mile, sir.

Senator Newlands. You heard the cries of the people in the water, did you not?

Mr. Moore. Yes, sir; everybody heard that, sir.

Senator Newlands. Did you see the ship go down?

Mr. Moore. Yes, sir.

Senator Newlands. What was the appearance of the ship at that point of time?

Mr. Moore. I saw the forward part of her go down, and it appeared to me as if she broke in half, and then the after part went. I can remember two explosions.

C. E. Andrews, Steward in Lifeboat 16

Senator Bourne. How far were you from the Titanic at the time?

Mr. Andrews. I should say about half a mile, sir.

Senator Bourne. Did you see the Titanic sink?

Mr. Andrews. Well, sir, she must have been halfway sinking when I saw her.

Senator Bourne. Did you hear any explosion or noise?

Mr. Andrews. I heard just a small sound, sir; it was not very loud, but just a small sound.

Senator Bourne. Did you think that the ship broke in two?

Mr. Andrews. That I do not know, sir. When we got away in the boat at the last, everything seemed to go to a black mist. All the lights seemed to go out and everything went black.

Frederick Clench, Seaman in Lifeboat 12

Senator Bourne. Did you see the ship sink?

Mr. Clench. Yes, sir.

Senator Bourne. About a quarter of a mile away?

Mr. Clench. About a quarter of a mile away.

Senator Bourne. Did she sink bow down?

Mr. Clench. Bow down; yes, sir.

Senator Bourne. Did she break in two?

Mr. Clench. That I could not say.

Can these really all be confirmed eyewitness accounts of survivors? Some of them claim the Titanic split in two before sinking, some claim it sank intact, and some are unsure. Many others didn't comment on whether it split before sinking during their interviews. In fact, of those interviewed, 4 survivors claimed the ship split in two, 13 claimed it sank intact, and 65 either didn't know or didn't comment on it.

How can that be? They all saw the same event from their lifeboats, but their statements contradict. Those statements are...

Exactly what you'd expect of eyewitness testimony.

According to investigative experts, multiple independent eyewitnesses rarely see all the same details and will never describe the event in the exact same words.[2] Agreement on the major event with differences in the minor details is the very nature of eyewitness testimony. In other words:

Divergent details actually strengthen the credibility of eyewitness testimony.

Now check out these eyewitness accounts that describe the same event:

From Matthew's Gospel: *After the Sabbath, at dawn on the first day of the week, Mary Magdalene and the other Mary went to look at the tomb. There was a violent earthquake, for an angel of the Lord came down from heaven and, going to the tomb, rolled back the stone and sat on it. His appearance was like lightning, and his clothes were white as snow. The guards were so afraid of him that they shook and became like dead men."* [3]

Now from Luke's Gospel: *"On the first day of the week, very early in the morning, the women took the spices they had prepared and went to the tomb. They found the stone rolled away from the tomb, but when they entered, they did not find the body of the Lord Jesus. While they were wondering about this,*

2. I Don't Have Enough Faith to be an Atheist, Frank Turek

3. Matthew 28: 1-4

suddenly, two men in clothes that gleamed like lightning stood beside them."[4]

How can that be? Those statements contradict! Those statements are...

Exactly what we'd expect from eyewitness testimony.

First of all, the two passages don't actually even contradict one another. Matthew's Gospel doesn't say there was **only** one angel. Matthew could have chosen to mention just one for any number of reasons.

That said, even if there was an apparent contradiction, we know that divergent secondary details *strengthen* the testimony. It shows the gospel writers didn't get together to smooth out the differences in their accounts. It should not be a surprise that the gospels aren't word-for-word copies of one another. They contain specific details that are unique to each eyewitness. They were written for different purposes and with different audiences in mind. [5]

- Matthew, one of the twelve Apostles, wrote his gospel to a Jewish audience. It demonstrates that Jesus is the promised Jewish Messiah.

- Mark's gospel is the shortest of the group. It's the record of the Apostle Peter's eyewitness observations, written by his translator and disciple.[6] It is structured around Peter's preaching style, not neces-

---

4. Luke 24: 1-4

5. Voddie Baucham- Why I Believe the Bible

6. Chapter 5 of J Warner Wallace's "Cold-Case Christianity" is a fascinating study on this issue.

sarily putting the events in chronological order.

- Luke, as previously mentioned, was a meticulous historian. His goal was to write an "orderly account" based on various eyewitnesses including the Apostle Peter, and Mary, the mother of Jesus. He focuses on chronology and history.

- John, Apostle and eyewitness, wrote his gospel for evangelism. It is structured around seven major signs.

Multiple independent eyewitness accounts can be pieced together to help get a fuller picture of the story. There is even a phenomenon that occurs called "undesigned coincidences." This describes instances where a detail in one writer's account inadvertently clarifies a point in another writer's account. For example, the gospel of Matthew records Jesus pronouncing judgment on Bethsaida, "*Woe to you, Bethsaida! For if the mighty works done in you have been done in Tyre and Sidon, they would have repented long ago...*"[7] The question is – what mighty works were done in Bethsaida? Matthew doesn't mention any. However, the Gospel of Luke fills in the gap. Luke mentions that Jesus feeding the 5,000 happened in Bethsaida.[8] The Bible is full of these "undesigned coincidences." Cambridge Professor JJ Blunt identified at least sixty of these in the New Testament documents alone.[9] And that's the beauty of having multiple eyewitness accounts. We can piece them together to get a fuller picture of the story.

---

7. Matthew 11:21

8. Luke 9:10

9. Stealing from God- Frank Turek

Let's head back to the Titanic to put a bow on this thought. The survivors of the ordeal all agreed on the major event that, the ship had sunk. Whether it split in two or went down intact doesn't change that. Likewise, the Gospel writers all agreed on the major event - that Jesus rose from the dead. Whether there was one angel or two at the tomb on Sunday morning, doesn't change that fact.

We're ready to send this one up to the Chief for signoff.

Referral: The Bible isn't reliable because it's full of contradictions.

CUO Approval: "Therefore everyone who hears these words of mine and puts them into practice is like a wise man who built his house on the rock. The rain came down, the streams rose, and the winds blew and beat against that house; yet it did not fall, because it had its foundation on the rock." [10]

---

10. Matthew 7:24

Chapter Seventeen

"BUT THE BIBLE PROMOTES VIOLENCE, GENOCIDE, AND SLAVERY..."

O n March 24, 1972, Amil Dinsio and his crew pulled off the perfect robbery. This was a professional job. It was also a family affair; with Dinsio's brother, nephew, and brother-in-law, among his co-conspirators. The crew included:

- Amil Dinsio- mastermind of the operation

- James Dinsio- explosives specialist and designer of burglary tools

- Phil Christopher- security alarm specialist

- Charles Mulligan- getaway driver

- Charles Broeckel- muscle

Dinsio and his Youngstown, Ohio-based crew practiced for months before flying out to California for the job. Their target was a bank, in which it was believed that President Richard Nixon kept a multi-million-dollar rainy day fund. The crew used dynamite to blast a hole through the roof of the concrete vault, disarmed the alarm, and made off with over $12 million worth of cash and valuables. Then, they scrubbed down the townhouse they had rented to serve as their head-quarters and returned to Ohio undetected.

If they'd stopped there, they might have gotten away with it. But the crew made the mistake of pulling a similar job in Ohio months later. Ultimately, the FBI linked the two robberies, and flight records placed the crew in California at the time of the first job. An initial search of the townhouse revealed nothing until the dishwasher was checked. The crew had forgotten to run the dishwasher before leaving, and their fingerprints were recovered on the contents inside. Ultimately, the entire crew was arrested and convicted.

Now, let's change the details. Suppose someone had an account at that bank with $12 million in it. Would they also be arrested if they walk in and make a $12 million withdrawal? Of course not. It's their money.

And this, friend, leads us to our next referral. Stay with me here. Many object to the Bible on the grounds that it "promotes violence and genocide". They point mainly to the Old Testament. Two of the most common examples would be the great flood in Genesis (Noah's Ark), and God's command to destroy the Canaanites in Deuteronomy.

There are entire books dedicated to the intricacies of each unique situation, [1] but let's start with the fact that God cannot commit murder. That's like comparing a legitimate bank transaction to the Dinsio heist. God is the rightful account holder of this universe. There's nothing wrong with a legitimate bank withdrawal because; (1) it's the account-holders money to begin with, (2) they put it in the bank, and (3) they can withdraw it whenever as they see fit. Likewise, God can't commit murder because; (1) He created us all in the first place, (2) He put us in the world, (3) He can withdraw us out of the world as He sees fit. For the record, abortion would be akin to the Dinsio heist.

With this in mind, the objection falls on its face immediately. But it's important we take it a step further. Events such as the great flood or the destruction of the Canaanites aren't arbitrary, random acts – *they're judgment.* The flood was a judgment for the wickedness of the human race since *"every inclination of the thoughts of the human heart was only evil all the time."*[2] As for the Canaanites, they had been doing absolutely vile things for 400 years leading up to their judgment. For example, they would sacrifice their babies to a false god called *Molek.* They would heat up this metal statue, place their babies in the arms of the figure, and watch the babies sizzle to death. The drummers in the village would play their drums extra loud, so the parents didn't hear the screaming.[3]

God put an end to it.

---

1. See Paul Copan's "Is God a Moral Monster?"

2. Genesis 6:5 NIV

3. Frank Turek- God a Moral Monster?

When brought out into the light of context, a claim that the Bible "promotes violence and genocide" makes very little sense.

The same could be said about slavery. Critics allege that the Bible "condones slavery". Really? This is why Greg Koukl advises to, "Never read a Bible verse. Instead, always read a paragraph at least." We need context. If a scripture seems like it's the antithesis of thousands of years of Christianity, it's likely we are misunderstanding the verse. For one, the slavery in the Old Testament isn't like the slavery we think of today. We generally think about the slave trade that ended less than 200 years ago here in the United States. We think of race-based slavery with people being kidnapped and enslaved against their will. But in the Old Testament, kidnapping is punishable by death, and slavery had nothing to do with race. The slavery in the Old Testament would be more like what we think of as, indentured servitude. People voluntarily became servants as a means to pay off debt and have a roof over their heads while they did it.[4]

Again, there are books like *Is God a Moral Monster?* by Paul Copan that are dedicated to examining the intricacies of these type of issues. For our purposes, we can see that to object to the Bible on moral grounds is nonsensical. Jesus took human morality to its highest plain. We have what we need to refer this up to the Chief.

Referral: The Bible isn't reliable because it promotes violence, genocide, and slavery.

CUO Approval: *"Blessed are you when people insult you, persecute you and falsely say all kinds of evil against you because of*

---

4. Slavery and Genocide in the Bible- Answered by Dr. Frank Turek

me. Rejoice and be glad, because great is your reward in heaven, for in the same way they persecuted the prophets who were before you." [5]

***

Chapter Eighteen

"BUT ONLY UNEDUCATED REDNECKS BELIEVE..."

"In regard to this Great Book, I have but to say, it is the best gift God has given to man. All the good the Savior gave to the world was communicated through this book. But for it, we could not know right from wrong. All things most desirable for man's welfare, here and hereafter, are to be found portrayed in it."

I f asked for the source of this quote, many people today would say that these are clearly the words of a religious fanatic.

This fanatic regards the Bible as though it is literally the authoritative word of God - as if it's the universal standard for morality and the foundation upon which society must be built to prosper. In other words, the author is a primitive, uneducated fool who doesn't know any better. Since the United States was built on a strict separation of church and state, we can dismiss dangerous religious ideas like those found in the Bible.

Friend, there's a technical term for this line of thinking. It's called **wrong.**

Dead wrong, actually. Are you ready for the identity of the author of this quote? Our uneducated, bigoted redneck is....

Abraham Lincoln.

Yup. *That* Abraham Lincoln. President Abraham Lincoln. Commander in Chief Abraham Lincoln. Liberator of slaves Abraham Lincoln. Our mystery man with the suspect moral compass is known as "Honest Abe," for crying out loud. And he's not the only Commander in Chief to have opined on the Bible. You might even say that our country is built on the Bible: [1]

- **John Quincy Adams, 6th President of the United States** - "So great is my veneration for the Bible and so strong my belief that when duly read and meditated upon, it is of all the books in the world, that which contributes most to make men good, wise, and happy."

- **Andrew Jackson, 7th President of the United States-** "That Book, sir, is the Rock on which our Republic rests."

- **Ulysses S. Grant, 18th President of the United States -** "My advice to Sunday Schools, no matter their denomination, is: Hold fast to the Bible as the sheet-anchor of your liberties; write its precepts in

---

1. https://www.christianheadlines.com/

your heart and practice them in your lives. To the influence of this book we are indebted for all the progress made in true civilization, and to this we must look as our guide in the future."

- **Theodore Roosevelt, 26th President of the United States -** "A thorough knowledge of the Bible is worth more than a college education."

- **Woodrow Wilson, 28th President of the United States** - "The Bible is the one supreme source of revelation of the meaning of life, the nature of God, and spiritual nature and needs of men. It is the only guide of life which really leads the spirit in the way of peace and salvation. America was born a Christian nation. America was born to exemplify that devotion to the elements of righteousness which are derived from the revelations of Holy Scripture."

- **Calvin Coolidge, 30th President of the United States -** "The strength of our country is the strength of its religious convictions. The foundations of our society and our government rest so much on the teachings of the Bible that it would be difficult to support them if faith in these teachings would cease to be practically universal in our country."

- **Harry Truman, 33rd President of the United States** - "The fundamental basis of this nation's laws was given to Moses on the Mount. The fundamental basis of our Bill of Rights comes from the teachings we get from Exodus and Saint Matthew, from Isaiah and Saint Paul.... If we don't have a proper fundamental moral background, we will finally end up with a totalitarian government which does not believe in rights for anybody except the State!"

- **Ronald Reagan, 40th President of the United**

States - "If we trust in Him, keep His word, and live our lives for His pleasure, He'll give us the power we need – power to fight the good fight, to finish the race, and to keep the faith."

Throughout the history of the United States, the single highest office in the country has been occupied by Bible-believing Christians. That includes our leaders in the 21st century. And it's not just political leadership. [2]

- **Francis S. Collins, Ph.D. from Yale and MD from the University of North Carolina at Chapel Hill** – *"The God of the Bible is also the God of the genome. He can be worshipped in the cathedral or in the laboratory. His creation is majestic, awesome, intricate and beautiful - and it cannot be at war with itself. Only we imperfect humans can start such battles. And only we can end them."*

- **Hugh Ross, Ph.D. in Astronomy, Astrophysicist-** *"I especially enjoy integrating the content of the Bible—all 66 books—with the findings reported in multiple science journals. This process leads to fresh insight and application."*

- **Stephen C. Meyer, Ph.D. in Philosophy of Science from Cambridge** – *"I think many discoveries of modern science have positive, faith-affirming implications, including the discovery that the universe, time, and space had a beginning; that the laws and constants of physics are finely tuned to allow for the possibility of life; and that biological systems display striking evidence of design, in particular, the molecular machinery and digital*

2. Christians in Science and Tech

information we find in living cells. It's a great time for Christians to work in science."

- **Alister McGrath, Doctor of Philosophy for Research in Molecular Biophysics, Cambridge** – *"Tradition is a willingness to read Scripture, taking into account the ways in which it has been read in the past. It is an awareness of the communal dimension of Christian faith, which calls shallow individualism into question. There is more to the interpretation of Scripture than any one individual can discern. It is a willingness to give full weight to the views of those who have gone before us in the faith."*

- **Ian Hutchinson, Ph.D. in Engineering Physics, Nuclear Engineer and Physicist at the Massachusetts Institute of Technology** – "I take the Bible very seriously. I take it seriously, and would affirm the the notion that it is inspired by God and profitable for teaching, reproof and correction as it says in 2 Timothy 3:16. But that doesn't mean that when we come to it, our particular interpretations are always affirmed by God."

Friend, this list doesn't even constitute a drop of a drop in the bucket. Some people seek to summarily dismiss the Bible as something only believable to people who "don't know any better". That's nonsense. You sure don't *need* a Ph.D. to find G-O-D, but countless people have them and believe.

Referral: "Only uneducated rednecks believe the Bible."

CUO Approval: *"You are Israel's teacher,' said Jesus, 'and do you not understand these things? Very truly I tell you, we speak of what we know, and we testify to what we have seen, but still, you people do not accept our testimony. I have spoken to you of* *earthly things and you do not believe; how then will you believe if I speak of heavenly things?"* [3]

***

---

3. John 5: 10-12

Chapter Nineteen

"BUT THE BIBLE IS SEXIST..."

"Wives, submit yourselves to your own husbands as you do to the Lord. For the husband is the head of the wife as Christ is the head of the church, his body, of which He is the Savior. Now as the church submits to Christ, so also wives should submit to their husbands in everything."

This is exactly the type of verse that is loved by people who hate the Bible. "See! The Bible is sexist! It tells women that they need to be submissive to their husbands." It's the type of verse that makes for creative anti-Christian memes that can be shared online. But is it true? Is the Bible really sexist?

To tackle this claim, I consulted the work of several of the leading women in Christian Apologetics – namely Alisa Childers (Another Gospel), Dr. Rebecca McLaughlin (Confronting Christianity), and Hillary Morgan Ferrer (Mama Bear Apologetics).

This issue always starts at the beginning. Yes, the beginning, as in the beginning of humanity itself. The creation account is found in the first book of the Bible, Genesis.

"When God created mankind, he made them in the likeness of God. He created them male and female and blessed them. And he named them, 'Mankind' when they were created."[1]

This cannot be understated:

Women and men were both created in the image of God.

This underpins the entire Christian worldview. This is why there is inherent dignity and equal worth in ALL human life. Consider this:[2]

- It is estimated that between 15,000 and 50,000 women and children are forced into sexual slavery in the United States every year. Unfortunately, this is difficult to track, and some reports estimate as many as 300,000.

- According to the National Center for Missing and Exploited Children, 10,000 prostitutes were brought to Miami for the 2010 Super Bowl. This is commonplace for large sporting events loaded with tourists.

- 30% of global human trafficking victims are children.

---

1. Genesis 5: 1-2

2. Thehighcourt.co

Do those stats make you sick to your stomach? If so, why? Chances are, you don't know these women and children. You don't know their names, you don't know what they look like, you don't know what type of life decisions they've made, you don't know what their individual circumstances are, or what mistakes they've made in their lives. You don't really know anything about them.

You don't need to. Do you?

Of course not. And the reason is that those things aren't what dictates someone's value. There is inherent dignity in ALL human life. That dignity comes from our Creator and is affirmed in the Bible.

With the creation account as our starting point, let's next look at Jesus. We know Jesus taught that the Bible is the authoritative word of God, more important to us than physical sustenance. So, if the Bible is sexist and Jesus endorses it, then by definition, that makes Jesus Himself sexist. Does that sound consistent with anything you've ever known or heard about Him? Consider this account:

"Jacob's well was there, and Jesus, tired as He was from the journey, sat down by the well. It was about noon. When a Samaritan woman came to draw water, Jesus said to her, 'Will you give me a drink?'(His disciples had gone into town to buy food). The Samaritan woman said to him, 'You are a Jew and I am a Samaritan woman. How can you ask me for a drink?' (For Jews do not associate with Samaritans). Jesus answered her, 'If you knew the gift of God and who it is that asks you for a drink, you would have asked Him and He would have given you living water... everyone who drinks this water will be thirsty again, but whoever drinks the water I give to them will never thirst. Indeed,

the water I give them will become in them a spring of water welling up to eternal life." [3]

We see this over and over again. Jesus defied first-century cultural norms to elevate women. He lifted human morality to the highest plain in history. For instance:

1. **The cultural norm was that, only women were held accountable sexually.** But Jesus taught, *"You have heard that it was said, 'You shall not commit adultery.' But I tell you that anyone who looks at a woman lustfully has already committed adultery with her in his heart."* [4]

2. **Education of women was strongly discouraged.** But in the house of Mary and Martha, Mary sat at Jesus' feet, listening to what He said. To "sit at the feet" of a Rabbi and learn was a place of honor. When Martha protested that Mary wasn't helping with the labor, Jesus tells her *"Mary has chosen what is better, and it will not be taken away from her."*[5]

3. **The testimony of women was not even admissible in Jewish courts**. Yet, it was women who Jesus revealed the empty tomb to first. It was those women who the risen Jesus appeared to first, and it was those women who were the first to share the good news! [6]

---

3. John 4: 7-10, 13

4. Matthew 5:27

5. Luke 10: 42

6. Matthew 28: 1-10

Jesus respected and honored women, so it should not come as a surprise that the early church also did. We find teaching in the Bible that was considered absolutely radical in first-century Jewish culture. For instance, the Apostle Paul taught that not only does a woman's body belong to her husband, but the husband's body belongs to his wife. This was unheard of at the time, and it leads us back to a recurring theme: never read a Bible verse. Always read a paragraph, at least. [7]   Let's return to the excerpt we opened this chapter with. This time, we'll read the entire section.

Instructions for Christian Households

Submit to one another out of reverence for Christ. Wives, submit yourselves to your own husbands as you do to the Lord. For the husband is the head of the wife as Christ is the head of the church, his body, of which He is the Savior. Now as the church submits to Christ, so also wives should submit to their husbands in everything. **Husbands, love your wives, just as Christ loved the church and gave Himself up for her to make her holy, cleansing her by the washing with water through the word, and to present her to Himself as a radiant church, without stain or wrinkle or any other blemish, but holy and blameless. In this same way, husbands ought to love their wives as their own bodies. After all, no one ever hated their own body, but they feed and care for their body, just as Christ does the church – for we are members of his body. For this reason, a man will leave his father and mother and be united to his wife and the two will become one flesh. This is a profound mystery – but I am talking about Christ and the church. However, each one of you also must love his wife as he loves himself, and the wife must respect her husband.** [8]

---

7. Greg Koukl

8. Ephesians 5: 21-33

It reads a little different in context, wouldn't you say? The so-called "sexist" passage instructs husbands to love their wives as Jesus loves the church – a sacrificial love, just as Jesus gave Himself up for us as believers.

Listen – there are challenging verses throughout the Bible, especially in the Old Testament. The Bible does not shy away from portraying some awful things done by humans throughout history – rape, incest, polygamy, and all sorts of other sins against women. These things are in the Bible to condemn sin, not endorse it.

Let's refer this one up to the Chief and press on, friend.

Referral: The Bible is sexist.

CUO Approval: *"The proud religious law-keepers came to Jesus. They tried to trap Him by saying, 'Does the Law say a man can divorce his wife for any reason?' He said to them, 'Have you not read that He who made them in the first place made them man and woman? It says, 'For this reason a man will leave his father and his mother and will live with his wife. The two will become one.' So they are no longer two but one. Let no man divide what God has put together."*

Chapter Twenty

"BUT SO MANY SMART PEOPLE DON'T BELIEVE..."

The TV show, *Mad Men,* is set on Madison Avenue, New York City, in the 1960s. In some ways, it seems like a completely different American society than we live in today. For one thing, just about every character in the show is constantly smoking. A doctor even strolls into the exam room to perform an appointment with a cigarette in his mouth in one striking scene.

It's hard to imagine. But they didn't know any better back then. They didn't yet have the information about the health risks. Today is a different story. We know that smoking causes cancer, diabetes, and all sorts of other diseases. We also know that there's a huge financial cost associated with smoking, both individually and societally. In short, we have overwhelming evidence that smoking is awful.

Thankfully, with all of this information, we now have zero smokers in the United States.

Oh, wait! That's not right. Cigarette smoking is still the leading cause of preventable disease and death in the country. Nearly half a million people will die from smoking-related causes this year. That's more than HIV, illegal drugs, alcoholism, car accidents, and firearms *combined*. Another 16 million people will suffer from diseases caused by smoking cigarettes.[1]

How can this be? We've known about the health risks for decades. There have been explicit warnings on cigarette packages since 1966:

WARNING: Tobacco smoke can harm your children.
WARNING: Tobacco smoke causes fatal lung disease in nonsmokers.
WARNING: Smoking causes head and neck cancer.
WARNING: Smoking causes bladder cancer, which can lead to bloody urine.
WARNING: Smoking during pregnancy stunts fetal growth.
WARNING: Smoking can cause heart disease and strokes by clogging arteries.
WARNING: Smoking causes COPD, a lung disease that can be fatal.
WARNING: Smoking reduces blood flow, which can cause erectile dysfunction.
WARNING: Smoking reduces blood flow to the limbs, which can require amputation.
WARNING: Smoking causes type 2 diabetes, which raises blood sugar.
WARNING: Smoking causes age-related macular degeneration, which can lead to blindness.
WARNING: Smoking causes cataracts, which can lead to blindness.

---

1. Smoking stats from FDA.gov

Do those messages strike you as unclear? Of course not. Smoking is no longer simply a "lack of information" problem. So, what is it? Does it come down to smarts? Surely, no intelligent person would take up a super-harmful and super-addictive habit in this day and age.

Well, our country elected a President who did. President Barack Obama wrote in his memoir that he continued to smoke 8-10 cigarettes a day *while serving in the White House.*[2] Whether you love or hate his politics, this is an objectively intelligent man. He ascended to the highest office in the country yet still engaged in a terrible habit.

The bottom line is, smoking isn't purely a matter of intelligence. There is overwhelming evidence that smoking is terrible, yet plenty of brilliant people have chosen to do it. Likewise, there is overwhelming evidence that the Bible is true, yet plenty of brilliant people choose not to believe. I've encountered countless people in my life and could not understand their unbelief – "he's such a nice guy, he's such a smart guy, how can he not see it?"

As perplexing as this may seem, we shouldn't be surprised.

The Bible tells us that unbelief isn't an intelligence problem – it's a spiritual problem.

"What we have received is not the spirit of the world, but the Spirit who is from God, so that we may understand what God has freely given us. This is what we speak, not in words taught us by human wisdom, but in words taught by the Spirit, explaining spiritual realities with Spirit-taught words. The person without the Spirit does not accept the things that come from the Spirit

of God, but considers them foolishness, and cannot understand them because they are discerned only through the spirit."[3]

And there it is. It doesn't matter how smart you are. If you haven't bent a knee and given your life to Jesus, you won't believe it. Unbelief isn't a lack of information; it's a lack of obedience. Just look at the 12 Apostles Jesus chose – it was a bunch of fishermen and a tax collector; full of flaws. This wasn't a collection of elite scholars. Meanwhile, nearly 40% of professors at elite universities like Harvard are atheists or agnostic. [4] Pathetic, but not unexpected.

We have what we need to refer this one up to the Chief. Let's roll.

Referral: The Bible isn't reliable because there are so many smart people who don't believe it.

CUO Approval: "At that time, Jesus said, '*I praise you Father, Lord of heaven and earth, because you have hidden these things from the wise and learned, and revealed them to little children. Yes, Father, for this is what you were pleased to do.*'"[5]

***

---

3. 1 Cor 2: 12-14

4. https://www.harvardmagazine.com/

5. Matthew 11:25-26

Chapter Twenty-One

CONCLUSION

I still remember the first time I heard it. I had recently given my life to Jesus, and everything was changing. I found myself in church, hungry to learn the Word of God. My Pastor read Hebrews 4:12, and it blew me away:

> *"The word of God is active and alive, sharper than any doubled edged sword."*

Whoa. It was as if a jolt of energy had shot through my body. His Word is alive! Of course, it is. We serve the one true living God.

Friend, the evidence that the Bible is true is overwhelming. It all starts with Jesus. Since Jesus is the Son of God, our view of the Bible is based on what He taught about it.

In Part 1 (Triage), we took the critical first step of triaging the 10,000+ religions on the planet. They can't all be true because they make conflicting claims. Therefore, we gave ourselves the best chance of finding truth by directing our efforts by the guidance of the Son of God. Our eligibility requirement is that the book(s) must be endorsed by Jesus Christ. Only the Bible passes this test, as Jesus taught it is more important than physical sustenance.

With the triage complete and only one holy text left standing, we were able to focus our efforts and crank up the heat on our review of the Bible. In Part 2 (Underwriting), we underwrote the text by taking a closer look at some specific risk characteristics. We found that the Bible is a **C**ollection, **O**ut in front of science, **R**esilient, **R**evered, **E**yewitness, **C**orroborated, and that there are **T**housands of manuscripts. In other words, the Bible is **CORRECT.**

Finally, in Part 3 (Referrals), we addressed common questions head-on. These issues were referred to the ultimate authority for approval. The words of Jesus Christ, our "Chief Underwriting Officer," served as signoff.

All that is left to do is consummate the deal and "bind coverage." We have all the information we could need, but all the evidence in the world can't change us. We're only made new when we put our faith in Jesus Christ alone.

I pray that this information is a blessing to you, my dear brother or sister in Christ. I pray that it helps strengthen your faith in this skeptical world and that it emboldens you to share the Good News of Jesus Christ with others.

Now, it's time for me to step out of the way and let the lion out of the cage.

> *The law of the Lord is perfect, refreshing the soul. The statutes of the Lord are trustworthy, making wise the simple. The precepts of the Lord are right, giving joy to the heart. The commands of the Lord are radiant, giving light to the eyes. The fear of the Lord is pure, enduring forever. The decrees of the Lord are firm, and all of them are righteous. They are more precious than gold, than much pure*

gold; they are sweeter than honey, than honey from the honeycomb. By them your servant is warned; in keeping them there is great reward. But who can discern their own errors? Forgive my hidden faults. Keep your servant also from willful sins; may they not rule over me. Then I will be blameless, innocent of great transgression. May these words of my mouth and this meditation of my heart be pleasing in your sight, Lord, my Rock and my Redeemer. [1]

---

1. Psalm 19: 7-14

TURN THE PAGE FOR MORE!

TURN THE PAGE FOR MORE!

REVIEW REQUEST

REVIEW REQUEST

If you enjoyed **The Bible Uncomplicated**, I'd sincerely appreciate it if you'd leave a review. Positive reviews, even if just a sentence or two, are a huge help to search results and credibility so other people can find this book. Thank you!

Review Amazon US.
Review Amazon Canada.
Review Amazon UK.
Review Amazon Australia

God Bless!

MORE BOOKS BY JAMES FINKE

MORE BOOKS BY JAMES FINKE

H AVE YOU READ THE ENTIRE ***CHRISTIANITY UNCOMPLI-CATED*** SERIES?

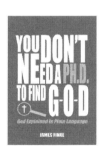

This book distills and deciphers the evidence that the God of the Bible exists. Are you ready? Let's talk God.

***

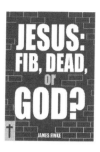

This book answers the most important question in history, asked by the most important person in history. Are you ready? Let's talk Jesus.

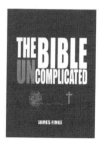

This book gives the business case for why we believe the Bible is the Word of God. Are you ready? Let's talk Bible.

***

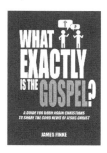

This book shares the most powerful message ever delivered on planet Earth. Let's talk Gospel.

BONUS MATERIAL

PLEASE ENJOY THIS SNEAK PEAK AT ANOTHER BOOK IN THE SERIES...

YOU DON'T NEED A PH.D. TO FIND G-O-D

God Explained in Plain Language

JAMES FINKE

YOU DON'T NEED A PH.D. TO FIND G-O-D

M y wife is a social worker by trade. I'm in the insurance business, so when she and her social worker friends talk shop, it can actually sound like a foreign language to me. *"I checked on the QRC, but his DZM was ABC."* You probably know the feeling. It could be mechanics talking cars, doctors discussing a procedure, whatever. If it's not your trade, they might as well be speaking Greek. You end up smiling and nodding, ready to move on to the next subject.

Does talking about God make you feel like an outsider listening to others "talk shop"? I'm convinced it is the case for many, whether or not they believe that God actually exists.

This is for you.

I'm not a pastor. I didn't go to seminary. Nor am I a professional scientist. Indeed, I've studied their work, but I couldn't write with their perspective even if I wanted to. It's kind of like, having a friend who's really into basketball. He may know his stuff, but he still isn't going to be slam-dunking if he's 5'2. I'm just a "regular guy" with the same fundamental question as you: **How do I find God?** The answer to that one question impacts and unlocks everything else in this life:

Is there a purpose for my life? Is there an afterlife? Will I someday see my friends and relatives again that have passed away? What religion is "right"? Is there a right and wrong way to live? Should I be going to church?

Now, most people accept that it takes faith to believe in God. But do you realize that it also requires faith to believe that there is no God? Faith is "the evidence of things we cannot see."[1] Right in the definition, we see that faith isn't meant to be blind. Just as our muscles can grow stronger through exercise, our faith to believe or not believe, can grow stronger through the study of the evidence.

This book is the result of my own study of the evidence. I've read, and I've listened to everything I could get my hands on from the top experts in the field. Experts in science, philosophy, history, religion, communication, and even crime investigation.

I've boiled it down and will share my takeaways as only a "regular guy" can. For example, I'll reference expert scientific research, but we won't get bogged down in hyper-technical scientific discussion. I'll also avoid using religious terms that would likely be foreign to those outside of the church.

I'm giving you the bottom line here and will share sources you can use to dive deeper into any of the topics we hit. If you want to know the intricacies of the second law of thermodynamics or to explore deep anagogical hermeneutics, there are plenty of places you can get that; it just won't be in this book.

Are you ready? Let's talk God.

---

1. Hebrews 11:1 NKJV

TO CONTINUE READING, DOWNLOAD HERE:

Amazon US
Amazon UK
Amazon CA
Amazon AUS

ABOUT THE AUTHOR

James Finke has spent the past 15+ years in Corporate America managing $50-million-dollar insurance portfolios. He is an expert in assessing risk and hedging bets. Therefore, it sometimes catches people off-guard when they discover he has gone all-in and wagered *everything* that the Bible is true.

His writing ministry began as a "quarantine project" for his church back in 2020. It has developed into a book series with thousands of copies in 13 countries and counting. The ultimate goal of the ministry is to glorify God and share the Gospel. Therefore, 100% of book proceeds are poured right back into advertising the *Christianity Uncomplicated* series around the world.

James lives with his wife and three young kids in Connecticut. He hosts a vibrant community of thousands of Christ-followers on his author page on TikTok. You can follow him at https://www.tiktok.com/@authorjamesfinke. You can also join the thousands of Christians who connect with James on email by signing up for his author newsletter at authorjamesfinke.com